CLOSED FOR
PRIVATE
FUNCTION

GW00673102

LIFE AS A PARTY

Also by Tina Brown

LOOSE TALK

Life As A Party

TINA BROWN

ANDRE DEUTSCH

To Michael and Miles

First published 1983 by
André Deutsch Limited
105 Great Russell Street WC1

Printed in Great Britain by
Ebenezer Baylis and Son Limited, Worcester

ISBN 0 233 97600 0

CONTENTS

ACKNOWLEDGMENTS

The author is grateful to the following people and organisations for permission to reproduce material from their collections: Alan Davidson for the photographs on pages 21 and 23; Betty Gallela for the photograph on page 120; Roxanne Lowit for the photographs on pages 86, 87 and 88; Chris Moyse for the photograph on page 133; Norman Parkinson for the photograph on page 123; Barry Swaebe for the photograph on page 50; Camera Press for the photographs on pages 27 and 80; the Press Association for the photograph on page 73; Syndication International for the photograph on page 48.

The photographs on pages 31, 53, 55, 60, 63, 68, 70, 74, 78, 90, 91, 93, 95, 98, 110, 136, 138, 141, 145, 151, 160 and 167 are reproduced by courtesy of The Condé Nast Publications Ltd. The author would like to thank in particular Mr Bernard H. Leser, Managing Director of The Condé Nast Publications Ltd, for his generosity in this regard.

The author also wishes to thank the following photographers: Clive Arrowsmith (page 140); David Bailey (pages 95 and 136); John Bishop (page 53); Nick Jarvis (pages 109, 112, 114, 116, 117 and 118); Dafydd Jones (page 90); Dudley Reed (pages 60, 63, 68 and 70); Victor Watts (page 74). The drawings on pages 38–47 and 125–135 are by Robin Ade. The drawing on page 149 is by John Spring.

Last note: Finally, the author wishes to thank Gabé Doppelt and Chris Garrett of *The Tatler* for their great help in organising this book.

HI, SOCIETY

I took over the editorship of the *Tatler* in June 1979, the same month that Mrs Thatcher took over Number 10. The upper classes were in an optimistic mood. 'At last,' the late Lady Hartwell commented at a Sunday lunch party, 'we're going to live in a world where we can sack people again.' Pundits started predicting the return to a smart, exclusive, well-mannered society.

Looking at the choice of available social coverage and what it said about England, I hoped they were right. As seen through the old *Tatler* most English parties seemed to be thrown at Madame Tussaud's. Each photograph featured some fresh tableau of the stiff upper rictus coming to terms with a glass of warm Amontillado. One particularly striking page in the *Tatler* headed 'The Butler Family Reunion' looked like a poster for *The Fall of the House of Usher*.

At the other extreme was the picture of social life in *Ritz*, David Bailey and David Litchfield's 'fashion and style' newspaper. Here it was all wide-angle flash-shots of over-excited hairdressers in fancy dress who bowled through the social year without so much as a passing nod at Ascot or the Caledonian Ball. Which was the truer picture of English Society? From where was this smart, exclusive, well-mannered etc. revolution going to come? There was a surge of hope when the Embassy Club in Bond Street re-opened. Social romantics dreamed of the whirl of bare shoulders fox-trotting with the patent-haired ghosts of Fort Belvedere days but this vision faded for me after I'd interviewed the new proprietors of the Embassy, former shirt-maker Michael Fish and his partner Jeremy Norman. 'Jeremy wanted a large, anonymous jump-up club with a homosexual clientele,' Fish said as we dined in a corner surrounded by large, anonymous homosexuals jumping up and down. 'We found the Embassy was up for grabs, but I said, Jeremy, you can't mix your metaphors. So we invited all the grand old nobs to the opening like Marg of Arg, Fruity Metcalfe and Maureen Marchioness of Dufferin and Ava who'd been in the same seats forty years ago at a party given by Douglas Fairbanks Sr. and just hoped they'd want to come back.'

Looking at the three black boys in lurex vests lassoing behind our table, it seemed an impractical concept.

But the new reactionaries were confident society was going straight. 'Poofs will be right out,' Lord Burghersh, 32, my new sporting correspondent, told me enthusiastically. 'The clientèle of the Embassy will have to cross a picket-line of abusive heterosexuals in Lucky Lucan moustaches. We're going to resurrect virility. We'll eat the butchest things on the menu like brains in brown butter instead of all this poncey Parma ham and melon.'

Lord Hesketh, 33-year-old squire of Easton Neston and eldest of three fat, fashionable brothers was more realistic. 'In 1979,' he told me, 'the way to tell an English gentleman is by the quality of his drugs.'

That summer, the interior designer Nicky Haslam gave a *tenue de chasse* ball in the grounds of his country house, at Odiham in Hampshire. It was a confident gesture. Lady Diana Cooper came as Diana the huntress and held court in an upstairs bedroom. The young buck Mark Shand painted himself and four friends black and white like a New York mugging gang and streaked back and forth through the jostling marquee. Lady Lambton wore a rubber diving suit and sat nose to nose with Joan Collins. Lord Hesketh found himself locked in a lavatory briefly. 'Is this a loo or a safe?' he hollered. Nigel Dempster sprang from table to table like a Demon Prince shouting 'Sauciness! Sauciness! I must find sauciness. I know it's somewhere in this tent!' At 2 a.m. a second wave arrived after attending a Greek shipping wedding in Paris.

I realised then that my struggle with the problem of how to reposition the *Tatler* as a society magazine was over. I was going to let them all into the party – the debs and the Eurotrash, the sporting and the snorting. From now on the editorial policy was to mix the Queen Mother with April Ashley – and make sure both of them had a good time.

But there was another problem. As editor of the *Tatler* one was ex-officio a member of Society. As a reporter one couldn't be. Since I was both, the magazine somehow had to accommodate the two of us. It was necessary to become a professional chameleon.

I was brought up in a way that made it easy. Home life was flash – my father was a film producer who managed to preserve his country gentleman air appropriate to his early productions of *The Chiltern Hundreds* and the first Agatha Christie films into the era when the art of setting up a film became Deals on Wheels. 'Who shall we have to dinner to massage the Iranian/Swiss/Belgian money?' was a catchphrase that signified the start of the school holidays. 'Everyone,' my mother would reply, 'and if he's anything like the Indian twenty per cent it better be a buffet.'

In the ensuing uproar everyone forgot about who the party was for. It didn't matter because he usually disappeared the next week anyway when the roof blew off his tax shelter. As far as I could see castles were always plaster, money was always funny and the nuns came off the set for a fag. By the time I went to boarding-school at the age of twelve, I fancied myself as a keen student of façade and kept a detailed diary.

But if home life was flash, school life was extremely proper. Hampden House, Great Missenden, where I finally ended up after being spat out, like a nail in a hoover, from a number of less flexible girls' academies was attended entirely by the daughters of *Country Life*.

While the other film babies went to groovy, progressive schools like Millfield or Bedales, I spent the next three years wearing a grey cloak with a Ku Klux Klan hood for Sunday morning walks and learning the piano from someone called Mrs Clotworthy. The solidity of the school's traditions was refreshing after the showbusiness world of jumping beans but some things appalled me. Compared to the warm razzamatazz of my own home I was always being surprised by the coolness of upper-class family life as glimpsed through the rareness of letters in the pigeon holes of my friends. On exeat Sunday the tea hall was always full of girls whose parents hadn't come to take them out. The upper-class marriage seemed to me to be characterised by a sort of electric indifference which gave their daughters low emotional expectations. Most of them married straight after doing the season in the fashionable spirit of embarrassment ('It's just to please Mummy really'), and found themselves trapped in a Fortnum & Mason hamper with a wan suspicion that the cartons were plastic. After their divorces they trudged around Sloane Street spending their money on imaginative table decor.

In the *Tatler* I invented a persona for dealing with my split perspective on their values – Rosie Boot – who wrote a monthly column about eligible bachelors. Rosie's literary stance was as a declared outsider whose assumptions about what girls want to know was unabashedly cynical. In short, does he have enough scratch to keep you up to scratch? When the column got into its stride, I used to get calls from ratty-voiced debs that began 'Look, I'd like to remain anonymous but I know this frightful shit you really ought to send Rosie Boot to interview.'

In the course of my research as Rosie I discovered that the Hooray Henry has never been in better form than now. Oxford dining clubs are packed with the heirs of the new Tory age getting 'hog-whimpering drunk'. They often appeared in the offices of *Tatler* at the end of their finals year offering to be investigative journalists. 'Look, I'm going to Tuscany next week with Pooter Blair – you know Pooter? Well, he's a terrific chap, a serious white man. Anyhow, I wondered if anyone had ever written anything about Harold Acton because I think Pooter's sort of got an open invitation.'

Young society, I discovered, is now almost permanently airborne. Not just on traditional up-market hops like Tuscany but long-hauling it to the Sydney social season in January, to Alaska for the salmon fishing in July, the Manhattan cocktail circuit in November. Traditional English events are often upstaged by more glamorous happenings across the Atlantic. 'Are there any Englishmen left in England?' wailed Jerry Zipkin, Nancy Reagan's walker, last summer. In June the Derby, for instance, is now mainly attended by feuding gossip columnists and rising jewellers while in August the erstwhile fun people at Cowes Week and the Dublin Horse Show now head for the glitzier zones of Long Island instead.

Only at Goodwood did I find the aroma of English class reassuringly preserved. Young swells held up binoculars like giant ice-cream cones and told each other, 'She's sweating a lot behind the saddle.' Girls wore red silk polka dot dresses with fluttering hems. Rumours floated on the sea breeze. 'I hear that Alastair's on the brink of marriage for the third time. He keeps marrying girls straight out of the *News of the World* then leaving them *exactly* where he found them.'

But the spirit of Concorde intruded again at Glyndebourne. 'I suppose,' mused a deb's delight throwing open his picnic hamper, 'opera is now the middle-class cocaine. Everyone here is paying 60 quid for a toot of *Rigoletto.*'

But while the souped-up Hooray Henry set formed the core of the *Tatler*'s new readers, we couldn't afford to lose the old.

Surprisingly, the people, who most vigorously entered into the spirit of the new double-edged *Tatler* were those I'd expected most to oppose it – a group I christened The Bright Old Things. Perhaps they were tired of being in *The Fall of the House of Usher* and liked the fashionable re-make. I was taken up by the golden oldies like the Hon Dolly Burns, Sir Iain Moncreiffe of that Ilk (who whipped his false teeth out at lunch at Langan's with the cry, 'Pretend it's a butterfly!') and the late Geoffrey Keating who constantly lured me to dinner parties which turned out to be *à deux*. Lady (Aliki) Russell, once Miss Athens in the 1930s, was another frisky septuagenarian whose face recurred with dizzying regularity as I pored over the light box looking at social snaps. A lunch party at her house in Chester Square was rich in other Bright Old Things. I was placed opposite one who, unless I misheard him, said he lived in Nostril Abbey. At the end of the table was the guest of honour, one of the brightest old things of all, Mary Duchess of Buccleuch. 'You've got that French man on your right at lunch,' she told me, indicating an ancient eminence with a hearing aid. 'The only thing I know about him is that he was a famous *aviateur* in the war and a collaborationist. They say he was responsible for having his mother-in-law turned into lampshades.'

'Was he a friend of Nancy Mitford's?' I asked (I had dined at Dolly Burns's the night before and the other guests all seemed to be writing biographies of the Mitfords).

'I doubt it,' shouted the Duchess. 'After the episode with the lampshades I'm afraid he was rather shunned by the smart set.'

My love-affair with the older generation reached its zenith, and some say its nadir, when I engaged Margaret Duchess of Argyll to write a gossip column. The idea was to upstage Betty Kenward, for decades Jennifer of Jennifer's Diary on *Harpers & Queen*, who kept sailing into the right parties ahead of *Tatler* like a giant powder-puff. It became a contest of coiffure. The Duchess, whatever her penchant for boosting the PR man of Philippine Airlines, cut a dramatic figure as she cruised out of the Grosvenor House where she lived, her hair dressed into crenellated ebony, her pale skin powdered like Marat. Mrs Kenward, on the other hand was an implacable meringue topped by a girlish black velvet bow. Unknowing hostesses who sat them together would sight them back to back, leaning on fists of kid leather. It was one of the thorns in the Duchess's side that the press never afforded her the same respect as Mrs Kenward, even though, as she kept insisting, they were both in the same profession. She phoned me constantly on this score, and sometimes appeared at my office in Bruton Street impeccable in a 30-year-old Chanel suit carrying her poodle, Alphonse. 'Some saucy monkey from the *Evening Standard* has been on to me asking how I'm paid. If he rings you, please send him packing.'

We finally licked the social coverage problem by inventing a diary section for the party pictures called Bystander whose emblem was the periwigged little red man from *Tatler*'s coffee-house history. But until the section reached its own level with its own editor, Miles Chapman, I often found myself either in hand-to-hand combat with importunate hostesses or scheming how to get one of our new team of young paparazzi behind closed doors. The upper-class hostess is schizophrenic. She longs for her party to be photographed as long as she is seen to have put every obstacle in the way of doing so. I learned to ignore her pleas for privacy after the hullabaloo when a rogue Instamatic brought back snapshots of the Duke and Duchess of Rutland's ball at Belvoir Castle, ('Saturday Night Belvoir' we called it) only to find that instead of a writ on publication we received a request for a free set of photographs. Collaboration, anyway, sometimes proved more nerve-wracking than piracy.

The saga of Mrs Eva Goodhew's head-dress gala at San Lorenzo was thirty yards of bad road. Mrs Goodhew, a sleek German blonde recently divorced from her MP husband and befriended by Pierre Trudeau ('The press are so cruel! They said because I lost the MP I went for the PM!') was determined that her head-dress gala should be the major social event of the summer season. Only the editor of the *Tatler* should be allowed to deal with the picture arrangements. 'I am very very worried about which head-dress shall I wear,' she often rang to say, 'the little bananas or the hat made out of cocktail olives?' But as time wore on she became more concerned about omens of a laissez-faire attitude among her guests towards the important head-dress theme. 'One of my friends rang up and said she will wear a garland in her hair. I said *absolutely not*. Surely you can make an effort? Can you not put some Christmas decorations on your head? Can you not festoon a birdcage and be a little *fou* with that? The British are so *lazy*. Only in Paris do they understand a party. Thank goodness there are some real people around like Aliki Russell. She asked me to find a very tall car for her to arrive in so I *know* she must be trying.'

The guest of honour was the Spanish ambassador. Mrs Goodhew was not amused when our photographer, the celebrated Tom Hustler, nearly strangled the castanet player with his electric lead, and had a sneezing attack all through the flamenco solo. Hustler, I came to realise, may achieve brilliant results but he has a talent for social over-kill. 'You asked if you could send a photographer and I open the door to a mountain. Electric leads! Flash guns! A regiment of assistants!' thundered Lord Weidenfeld when I'd persuaded him to let Hustler take 'one or two very discreet snapshots' of a private dinner for Henry Kissinger. Hustler, however, was as unfazed by this reception as he was by the beetroot face of the choking castanet player. He cruised through the room leaving a trail of upturned ashtrays stopping only to say 'How's tricks?' to Lord Carrington or give a thumbs up to the Governor of the Bank of England. 'Definitely not a full page here, dear,' he shouted at me as he crashed off into the night three hours later with a handful of cheese footballs.

I decided that what *Tatler* needed was a few scoops. It also needed to invent a new galère of social personalities. This was not as easy as it might seem. Glamour Queens, especially, are in particularly short supply nowadays. Dewi Sukarno, the still ravishing widow of the Indonesian dictator, was eager to get me to Paris to write about her exciting lifestyle.

When I arrived at the smart address in the Avenue Montaigne I found that Madame Sukarno lives alone with her daughter in a suite of shadowy rooms festooned with suspect Oriental mementoes and effusive Christmas cards. She kept excusing herself to make phone calls to 'Charles of the Litz'. It was not a scene to make the heart sing. Stars, stars, where were the stars?

I spent time cultivating a group I called the Footnotes. These were the people listed under their own name in the back of someone else's biography. They can often be spotted hovering round the new-book island in Foyles busy looking themselves up in the latest memoir. Sir Alfred and Lady Beit whom I encountered on an Irish tour are the archetypal Feetnote. They have known everyone from Fred Astaire to Oswald Mosley but never claimed the centre stage. As one of their estate hands at Russborough put it, 'Poeple might think the Beits are no longer in the social swim. But every so often a stiff invitation arrives from *you know where* and you know that in the places that matter the *Beits are not forgotten*.'

There are plenty of young feetnote coming up on the scene – many of them in the fashion world – and the point about them for an editor is that they lead one to the star. Manolo Blahnik, the exotic cobbler who owns Zapata where all the smartest girls buy their shoes is (no doubt, appropriately) a formidable Footnote. He is destined to be a relentless pass-through character in the biographies of Bianca Jagger, Paloma Picasso, Jerry Hall. With his slicked-back Chopin hair, Cosmopolitan origins and intimate knowledge of shoe-size his access is unbeatable. 'I love feet,' he told me once. 'If someone hes horrible feet I try and like them very much but I find it hard. The trouble with England is, too many people hef horrible feet. The whole blotter countrer is going to rot. You hef to give T.V. to the masses O.K. but there's another third and we are bored out of our minds.'

It was through the good offices of Manolo Blahnik *Tatler* got its cover picture and my close-up view of Princess Caroline of Monaco after repeated 'no's' from formal channels. A phone call to Zapata from fashion editor Michael Roberts confirmed that, yes, Her

Serene Highness was coming in to try on a pair of gold sandals. Our grovelling letter requesting the interview was secreted in the tissue-paper alongside the sandals, and success! From the humble beginnings of a Zapata shoe-box Roberts and I found ourselves whisked inside the peach-coloured portals of the Princess's house in Monaco.

Royalty-watching is a major preoccupation for the social journalist and so, perforce, is the watching of their friends. I was able to observe both in Mustique when I went to interview the Hon Colin Tennant and found Princess Margaret had just arrived on the island with her house party — Roddy Llewellyn and the NYC Venezuelan socialites Reinaldo and Carolina Herrera ('Busy, busy,' shrugs Reinaldo if one asks him what he does with his life). While Tennant played the outrageous entertainer clapping his hands to produce magic picnics and barbecues, the weekend never lost the latent unease of a royal presence. What, I asked one of the Mustique householders, do the royal party do all day? 'The same as everyone else,' he replied. 'Except in a slower, grander, duller way.' I felt that sensation again around Prince and Princess Michael of Kent when Princess Michael threw open the ornate doors to an enormous heirloom-stuffed room in Kensington Palace with the cry, 'This is our rumpus room'.

One discovers that the people who mix with royalty regularly, however relaxed and contemporary they seem, only survive as royal friends because they are, at heart, old-style courtiers. A year after I interviewed Colin Tennant on Mustique I went to Holkham Hall in Norfolk to do a piece on Lord Coke, then in the middle of a controversy about selling the Leonardo Codex. Holkham is the family seat of the Leicester family which Tennant married into. (His wife was born Lady Anne Coke.) The house where Lady Anne was brought up is an austere, high-minded Palladian palace in a windy park overlooking a lake inhabited by serious geese. The entrance hall, based on a Greek temple, has a vast ornate dome held up by columns of Derbyshire alabaster that look like swirling slabs of Windsor cheese. As I wandered through the freezing, funereal rooms I came across a wedding photograph displayed on a cordoned-off table. It was of Colin and Lady Anne Tennant, he freshly bald and very Fifties, she glacially blonde, with the Queen Mother and Princess Margaret sitting in the front row.

The antics of Mustique fell into a new perspective and I saw a dimension to the story I had missed at the time. It reminded me of the remark Tennant had made as he watched me watching Princess Margaret. 'I think there is a danger of being a little too amusing, don't you?'

We flirted with this danger regularly on the new, whacko *Tatler*. It was impossible not to offend some people inadvertently while deliberately risking the offence of others. One throw-away gag in a social caption could cost one the co-operation of the entire clan.

We never got it right, for instance, with the Fraser family. It went wrong early on in our coverage of them when a wag amongst the guests at the wedding of Lady Antonia's daughter Flora to Robert Powell-Jones made a lot of facetious jokes chronicled in our coverage about the quality of the wedding breakfast. After that, however hard I tried to rectify matters, every single brother or cousin or aunt of the Fraser family seemed to get it in the neck, *en passant*, in one part of the magazine or another.

Since the upper classes are all related, I sometimes dodged the flak with one interviewee only to find with mounting consternation I was talking to his cousin. After my Scottish trip to see the Thane of Cawdor, the Hon Robert Corbett was so incensed by my account of his bender with Rick Parker-Bowles, he wrote me a postcard which read, 'This is the worst instance of social betrayal since the massacre of Glencoe.' I never heard from Mr Parker-Bowles himself on the matter. I only learnt of his reaction when I did a piece on the Wiltshire set and called in on his brother.

Andrew and Camilla Parker-Bowles live in a house called Bolehyde Manor – pronounced, wouldn't yer know – Bullid. I turned up early one Saturday morning with the photographer Lord Moore en route to do a portrait of the Duke of Beaufort at Badminton. The Parker-Bowleses welcomed Derry Moore who had been in the Lifeguards with Andrew, now Colonel commanding the Blues and Royals, but when they realised they'd let the author of the Scottish piece into their sitting room they fell into a state of ill-disguised panic. With brilliant resourcefulness Derry burbled on about his time in the Lifeguards, fast running out of names.

'D'you remember old Chipper Briggs?' he'd try.

'Actually he's a Brigadier now,' Parker-Bowles would bark and an uneasy silence would fall. Finally, the vibes got so bad it seemed a good idea to move up the road and check out the Earl of Shelburne at Bowood. I felt sullen. 'Can I use your phone?' I asked Andrew who was giving me a hard stare. 'Only if you don't write an article about me like that hellish Scottish tour,' he burst out. I gave him a hard stare back. 'You won't know until it's too late,' I said viciously. After this candid exchange they posed in front of the fireplace with as many dogs and children as we wanted and I was able to observe that Camilla Parker-Bowles's friendship with Prince Charles had left her with all his speech mannerisms. 'Stowell Park? Oh, it's a brute of a hice but it has some virry virry nice pictures.' She redeemed herself at the end of the morning by describing the wife of a grand neighbour as 'Not tonight Josephine'.

It was the summer of the Royal Wedding so perhaps it was not surprising that the upper classes were in a highly strung mood. All Prince Charles's friends were anxious not to put a foot wrong with the unknown quantity Lady Diana Spencer before they knew whether they were in or out. (Out, as it transpired.) As far as the *Tatler* was concerned, Lady Diana provided an unlooked-for social bonanza that almost eclipsed the splendour of Mrs Eva Goodhew's head decor party. At last hostesses had a patriotic excuse to rattle the family rocks and fly in the steel bands. They all started jabbering again about the return of a smart, formal, exclusive, well-mannered Society. Watching the transformation of Lady Diana from a hesitant mouse into a glittering femme fatale was a source of fun and wonderment. She was an upper-class Cinderella starving herself, streaking her hair Hollywood blonde, taking her face to the best make-up artiste in town, flaunting bare shoulders at the opera, putting to rout the time-honoured traditions of royal dowdiness and, at the same time, all her tired old gossip-column rivals.

I met the Princess of Wales at the American Embassy a year later. She had become startlingly self-possessed, leading the small-talk with a slightly pointed chin, gallantly keeping each joke on its trapeze before gliding off on her new casters to the next palpitating group.

I liked to think Lady Diana's transformation was the keynote of the revamped *Tatler*. We too believed that a sense of fun and fashion did not mean kissing goodbye to the cruddier joys of stalking and salmon-fishing, and won the glossy seal of approval when Condé Nast, owners of *Vogue, House & Garden* and *Brides*, made it clear to our fearless proprieter Gary Bogard they would now like to add the *Tatler* to their stable. It was the first time Condé Nast had bought a new magazine title in Britain for 25 years. The sale took place in April 1982 and we moved from our honky tonk outpost in Covent Garden into Vogue House, in Hanover Square. It was a most respectable marriage.

That winter Rosie Boot attended a wedding reception in the City of London. All the grandest people in England were there, disgorging from shooting brakes and Rolls Royces to celebrate the union of a young Irish aristocrat and his bubble-faced bride. Roving the clusters of aunts, Rosie felt that so much eccentricity under one roof must be evidence of centuries of in-breeding. Hen-faced dowagers squawked at each other, middle-aged earls rummaged in their nostrils with napkin-sized handkerchiefs. A pterodactyl wearing a double row of pearls wheeled by on the arm of a baron with three stomachs. The chairman of an auction house ray-gunned his halitosis at a notoriously skint stately home owner. As she cruised each draughty, capacious hall looking for an eligible bachelor Rosie saw that waves of self-interest as much as blood united this enormous clan. No token hairdressers or cosmopolitan shoe designers had slipped in here. This was a serious wedding, a bona fide finger-buffet, the shape of smart, exclusive, well-mannered things to come.

Except of course, the joke was it had never gone away.

Outside it was freezing sleet and the lights of Big Ben, that corny, placemat view, lent the evening a Fifties timewarp feeling. I felt a stranger from a parallel present. Ms Boot was after a title. But what about me?

I went back to the office to look at the same faces on the projector where I knew I'd like them better.

In my three years of editing *Tatler* I had been Alice through the Lightbox. It was time to return to reality or find myself stranded – on the other side.

WHAT'S THIS PARTY FOR?

It was some time after midnight and the dance-floor was flashing with tiaras. A duchess boogied with a cabinet minister. A countess limboed underneath a judge. Outside in the floodlit garden the heir to a banking fortune relieved himself beside a statue. Inside at one of the younger tables a teenage Camilla in her mother's pearl choker and the scarlet silk ball-gown her grandmother wore to the opening of Diaghilev's Ballets Russes turned to her escort with a troubled stare. 'The thing I don't understand,' she hissed, 'is what this party's *for.*'

Little did the teenager realise she was present at a unique occasion — a private dance in a private house paid for by the host. Nothing was for sale, no one was touting for business. Small wonder she was confused. In her short party-going career one social theme — commerce — has emerged and stuck. A ball is no longer a ball. It's a ball-gown promotion.

Thus, as the recession hits private entertaining, the London social calendar becomes more frenetically mercantile by the day. The discerning guest can reel on a single evening from a jewellery bash at Les Ambassadeurs, to a cheese and wine soirée for a Japanese camera at Dial Nine, to a magazine launch at Heaven, to a Smirnoff freebie at the Travellers' Club and still get in a few hours sleep before going up in a balloon over cognac country at lunchtime the next day. The rage for up-market Tupperware parties reached its zenith last year when a PR company called Good Relations hit on the concept of joint hospitality. 'The Chairman of H.R. Owen and the Directors of the Panther Car Company request the pleasure of your company at a private viewing of the 1981 Summer Collection by Emanuel, Jewellery by Graff,' read the invitation.

'The concept was not so much cost-sharing as to build up H.R. Owen's glamour image by linking their cars with frocks and jewellery,' Good Relations told me. Five hundred guests turned up at the capacious room in Melton Court, including ITN's television cameras. Excitement reached boiling point when to the theme tune of *Chariots of Fire* the fashion show climaxed with the Emanuels' ivory silk taffeta wedding dress phut-phutting slowly up the red carpet athwart an H.R. Owen silver drop-head coupé.

'We were going to use a Panther de Ville,' said the Emanuels' PR of the time, Lindy Woodhead, 'but then we were afraid the exhaust fumes might asphyxiate the bride.' Miss Woodhead, who now represents such star fashion names as Cerruti, Oscar de la Renta, Krizia, Daniel Hechter, Louis Féraud and a Japanese fashion house called Soosa and Satsuma, sees joint-hosting as the promotional party trend of the future.

'The only thing to be careful about is who you enter into the marriage of convenience with. Obviously Cartier can't get into bed with, well, Top Shop, but one has to beat this recession somehow.' As hosts become more and more cunning at disguising sponsorship, guests at London parties amuse themselves with guessing the identity of the Mr Big behind tonight's placement. Paté de foie gras at home with a new burglar alarm? Harvey Wallbangers in association with designer chocolates and a rising young cigar? As for the flunkey, he was the prize in a Colman's Mustard Win-a-Butler competition.

The main point of all these parties is to generate good write-ups and good will, but unfortunately mere hospitality is no longer enough to win enthusiastic column inches from a blasé London press corps. An example of this was the saga of the lavish hype job done on a film called *Can't Stop the Music* starring Valerie Perrine and the Village People. It began with a lunch party at the Dorchester from which the gossip columnists rolled off to dismiss the film in a few offensive sentences (*Can't Stop the Mucus* was one suggested alternative title). They were greeted back a few months later to rubbish another luncheon at the Tower Hotel and then were

Streaming: *party boy Timothy Swallow does his Carmen Miranda numero*

positively garlanded with welcomes when they returned in dinner-jackets to quaff champagne in a marquee in Kensington and do a hatchet job on the première itself.

'Oh, they can be very ungracious, certainly,' said Jeffrey Lane, the tiny bald dynamo who controls the party lists for Rogers and Cowan. 'But what can one do? One loses a little more hair and tries harder. Fortunately there are some well-mannered people around. Angela Rippon couldn't come to the première of *An American Werewolf in London* but she wrote a charming letter and I'll certainly be inviting her again.'

'Trying harder' in PR parlance is to produce a guest or an angle tailor-made for journalists whose investigative ethos is 'follow that canapé'.

Sometimes the more elaborate stunts fail precisely because of the effort and time involved in attending them. How many bona fide journalists have time to trudge off to Bermans and get kitted out for some Bad-Taste Ball when the net result is a puff piece for lingerie? What manner of NUJ member is going to give up a week to board the Air Malaysia Jumbos destined for the opening of Wedgies club in Kuala Lumpur this April? It is more sensible to follow Jeffrey Lane's example and try for a guest so 'current' the press cannot afford to miss writing about the party. Chris Evert Lloyd on the night she won Wimbledon, for instance. Shirley Williams the night after the Crosby by-election. Miss World the night after the contest . . . 'I get sick of people who make snide remarks about some of our guests,' Jeffrey said. 'There is no such thing as rent-a-face. Only people who are invited and enjoy going out. We don't *end up* with Vivienne Ventura. She's a terrific guest, she talks a thousand languages and, now it turns out she's a friend of Julio Iglesias, she's quite hot as well.'

The fact remains, however, that the commercial spirit of London entertaining has thrown up an eerie new society of its own — a humming, hustling society whose members are listed in *Who Dat?* rather than *Who's Who*. It enjoys a parodic relationship with mainstream society rather as a Shakespearian subplot often mocks the serious action of the play. Thus its Nicholas Soames is Peter Langan. Its Tony Snowdon is Richard Young. Its Princess Margaret is Molly Parkin. Its Norman St John-Stevas is Ricci Burns. These are the stars who mingle with the Others — resting model girls with Uvasun tans, gay crimpers in lift-and-separate trousers, pancaked promotions stylists, tinted interior designers, pidgin-English shoe designers, disc-jockeys on the pull, fashion editors on the twirl, film stars on the wane, debutantes on the game, bon viveurs on the dole, peers of the realm on parole, all having a ball. They are no longer classified as fashionable bits of colour, as they were in the Sixties, reassuringly outnumbered by the Real Thing. They have taken over, big-banged, formed their own galaxy. In the face of their exploding heat, aristocratic society shrinks inwards or goes up for sale. Only Buckingham Palace remains aloof from the Casbah. The Prince and Princess of Wales are glow-worms illuminating a black hole in space.

Fifteen years ago the hairdresser Ricci Burns shot up-market when

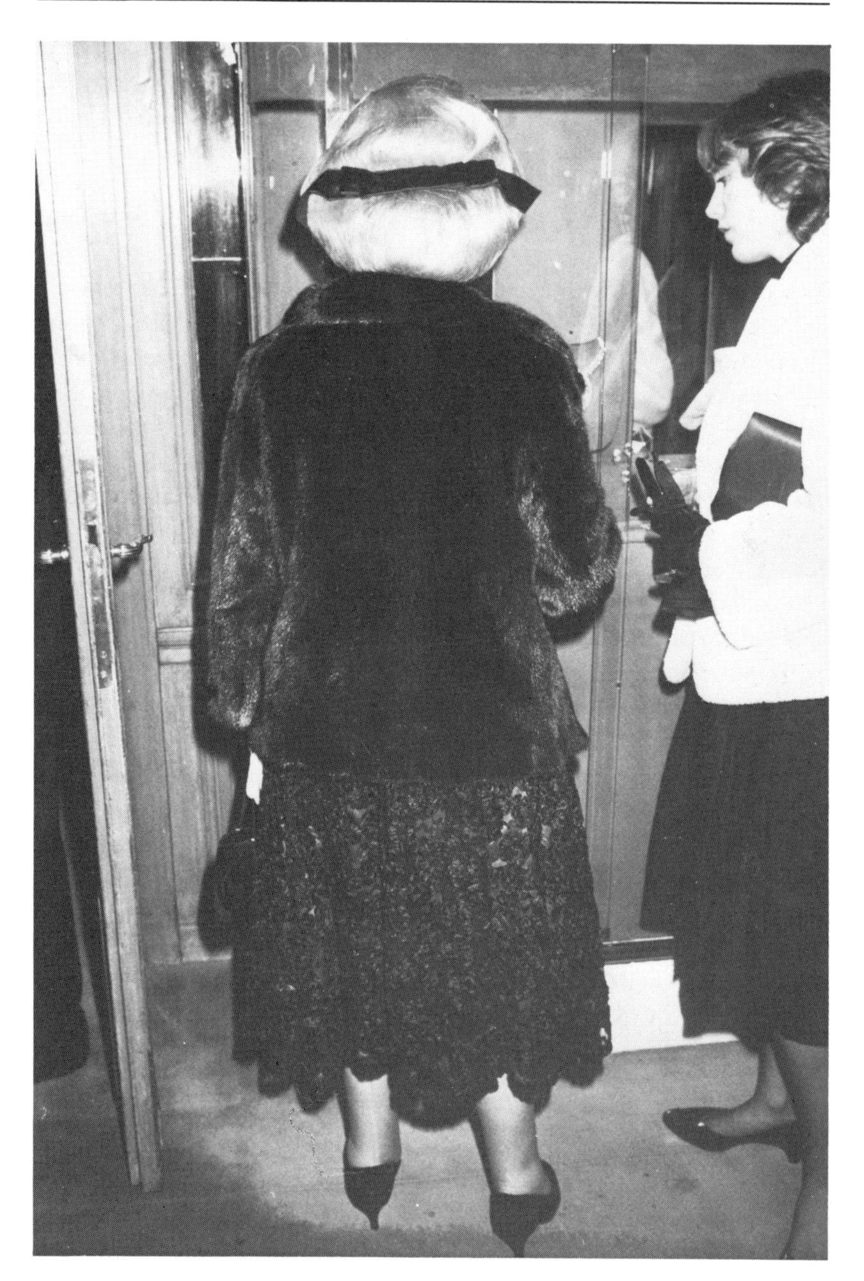

Over and out: *Betty Kenward (of Jennifer's Diary) really* has *to go on*

the meritocratic boom of the Sixties qualified him as 'fun to have around'. 'My forte was chignons so of course I got the glamour clients like Judy Garland. I remember taking her to the Ad Lib club one night. She started to sing and everyone told her to shut up. The Beatles were the only thing that mattered and being on banquettes 1 to 22 at the Ad Lib. It was a fabulous period.'

Today, however, Ricci is not the only hairdresser on the best banquette. Around him are a sea of blow-dry artistes from inferior salons. 'It's all become one big freebie with no style,' he complained. 'Even one's private entertaining isn't safe. The other evening after the Harry Winston party I went to dinner at Langan's with four friends. We were sitting there talking about the decadence of the New York art world when suddenly a man at the next table leant across and stole my roll! I love Peter Langan to die, but I don't know how he can let such people in! I said to the maître d' *forget it.*'

According to veteran houri Molly Parkin, however, whatever its changes in tone London is still a great improvement on New York. Molly has recently relaunched herself on the circuit after running out of life-story to fictionalise in her semi-pornographic semi-autobiographical novels. At fifty and recently divorced she has chummed up with the actress Jill Bennett and the two of them can often be sighted wearing outrageous hats in a raucous corner of the Caprice. 'In New York one always felt one had to be with the young,' said Molly, who was dressed for dinner that evening in a maroon taffeta chicken's leg originally made for a chorus girl playing a hen in a Tony Hancock sketch. 'Of course I miss my young lover, Ariel, a rock star, but I think he was the only heterosexual I met in the whole time I was there. And I hated the separateness of everything. The rich mixed with the rich, the pop world mixed with the pop world. Here I can enjoy a conversation with ageing barristers and TV celebrities in the same room as my daughter's young friends from St Martin's Art School and the National Theatre. Look at my friendship with Jill. When she says she went to Roedean, I say I went to Scrotum. That's London for you. A great melting pot.'

As anyone who's watched Molly Parkin in action knows, freebie society is possessed of a frantic energy. Its motor is ego even more than commerce. The conventional party aphrodisiacs of sex and drink and company are not relevant here. The party-giver may be selling a product but his guests are there to sell themselves. And self-promotion can make a deal with the strangest partners of all — face-lift at home with old-school tie and three year lease in Eaton Square. Alimony at home with good teeth and access to Princess Margaret. As Ricci Burns put it: 'To survive on the social scene you have to turn yourself into a package deal. Decide what your best points are and *be it, do it*,' Wonders, it seems, can be worked with unpromis-

Rosie Boot's Guide to London Bachelors

Hugo Page

Vote vote vote for Hugo Page. Or at any rate have dinner with him. At 29 he is clearly a rising young barrister with a keen interest in ladies' briefs but an even keener interest in the road to Number Ten. His father, Jack Page, is himself a Tory MP, and Hugo has fought two by-elections in Pontefract and Castleford in Yorkshire. He even became vice-president of the Pontefract borough football association, which seemed quite a coup until he discovered that most of his constitutents played rugger. Nonetheless, he acquitted himself dashingly on the hustings, winning all the hearts if not the votes, and it's not his fault that Pontefract is the tenth safest Labour seat in the country.

Hugo's only political flaw, it must be said, is not his stance on unemployment but his weakness for the opposite sex. No woman is deemed safe from 'pouncer' Page's indiscriminate enthusiasms. He has romanced some real dogs in his time and also some celebrated beauties, but friends claim he doesn't know the difference. Sex for Hugo is one long, victorious campaign.

How does he achieve his stunning success rate? Well, even his political opponents agree, Hugo is very personable. His Byronic black curls are always in romantic disarray and his long white silk scarf flutters behind him as if permanently followed by an off-stage wind-machine. He talks well too. Educated at Harrow and Cambridge, he knows the right psychological moment to bore his dinner dates into acquiescence with a sudden outburst of political philosophy. Then he'll whisk you back to his flat off the Gloucester Road in his yellow Morgan and ply you with plonk and proportional representation. Here, for the discriminating girl, the chief worry is the colour of his living-room. Impressed by an interior-decoration tip in a Sunday supplement, Hugo attacked the walls soon after he moved in with a concoction of brown and orange that produced an unfortunate dirty-protest decor. It turned his flatmate, Nicholas Monson, overnight into a passionate art collector.

Interior design apart, on the question of marriage Hugo's hot passions become coolly careerist. His wife is going to have to go down as well in Pontefract and Castleford as she does at dinner parties in Westminster — one reason perhaps why he has lately been courting the lovely Kate Asquith. Is Hugo out for the count? It's my belief that he'd settle down for the right political marriage but do remember girls, before you hit the campaign trail, a week is a long time in bed.

ing material. Take Timothy Swallow, the diminutive social meteor who works on the William Hickey column. What is Timothy Swallow's package? A stinging wit, at home with a mellifluous new voice, wild energy and a preposterous name. 'The new Society,' he told me, 'is invented by people like me who hankered for it from the provinces. I shall always be addicted to it because of that time working on the crumpet line and dreaming of what I'd wear to the première of *Valentino*. I still feel a surge of excitement when I come back to London after being away. All the people you keep seeing at these parties regard London as their life-support system that will save them from asphyxiation.

Thanks to our two leading paparazzi, Richard Young and Alan Davidson, everyone on the life-support system can hope for their fifteen minutes of fame, graduating, if they are lucky, from *Ritz* to Dempster's golden knock. Indeed their double act — Young with his morose black beard (catch-phrase: 'This is todally uneffical') and Davidson with his phlegmatic teddy-bear ears (catch-phrase: 'I was sitting there at the Turkish evening when my bleeper went') has come to be the trademark of the most popular freebie of the night. Young's photographs were recently compiled in a book called *By Invitation Only* and launched by Quartet at a thrash at Langan's Brasserie so hideously hybrid even Jeffrey Lane could not bring himself to attend. 'Why? Because it was wall-to-wall nobody. And if I want wall-to-wall nobody I stay at home and watch TV.'

In the middle of this personality souk, Ricci Burns begins to look quite low-key. 'London Society has had some bad knocks,' he said. 'First the upper classes packed up. Then the musicians packed up. Then the movie business packed up. So now don't ask who's picking up the tab and make the best of what you've got — *dross*.' As for the choice of the night's entertainment, would it be the Diana Dors record launch along with Adam and the Ants and a video crew at a brightly lit hangar in Kensington Park Gardens or the more cultural fine art freebie at the Francis Kyle gallery? *Forget it!* Nose job aloft, leather shoulders padded high, the pillar of the new Society swung off into the jostling neon night.

THE MUSTIQUE MYSTIQUE

what Colin Tennant does for Princess Margaret

Who is Colin Tennant? He is one of those people whose originality comes through the unsatisfying glimpses of the gossip columns. I think particularly of one striking photograph that's often reproduced of Tennant in a huge straw hat, his face alight with satirical charm. It seems to say, 'Watch me! I can carry anything off!' and sure enough his next appearance in the cuttings is in another wonderful hat, escorting his elder son, Charlie, to court when he was had up on a heroin charge.

The persona becomes all the more interesting in the light of the conventional litany of his *Who's Who* entry: *b* 1926; *s* and *heir* of 2nd Baron Glenconner; *m* 1956 Lady Anne Coke, *e d* of 5th Earl of Leicester; *educ* Eton; New College, Oxford; director, D. Tennant Sons & Co Ltd; until, suddenly, in 1967 we find C. Tennant chairman of a small dot in the Caribbean — Mustique, now famous as the holiday home of Princess Margaret. Ever since that entry, royalty watchers have been divided into two camps. Those who feel that Mustique saved Princess Margaret and those who feel it seduced her. Whichever side you are on depends on how you answer the question, 'What sort of man is Colin Tennant?'

My first sight of him is from the window of the six-seater plane as we swoop over a hill of waving palms and land at the festive little shack that constitutes Mustique airport. He is wearing white cheesecloth pyjamas with a stylish straw trilby and greets us with a wave. 'How kind of you to come!' he says, as his black driver, Austin, scoops up the bags and we bounce off in a jeep along a twisting dirt track. 'And a very good day, too, if I may say so. You see, Wednesday is our little jump-up, our gala evening at Basil's Bar when we put on a modest entertainment. Tonight the second act is a surprise.'

The first surprise, however, is Tennant himself. At 53, I had expected a much heavier man, a bon viveur with the gross flamboyance of an upper-class George Melly. In fact, his whole manner is one of impeccable understatement, and he is slim, nervous and quick. His face, with its pared profile, cynical mouth and blazing blue eyes shows an unsettling conflict between the intellectual and the hedonist.

The jeep stops at Tennant's house, a sort of mini Taj Mahal on the beach, looking out through palm-trees to the distant silhouette of the volcano on the island of St Vincent. Designed by Oliver Messel, who's since died, Tennant's palace is a romantic fantasy with domed roof, green and turquoise stained glass, carved doors, Moorish arches, and expanses of mushroom-coloured Italian marble. It is open on three sides with a parapet of green stones he brought back from China, tiling from Bali and an enormous sitting-room. The ceiling drips with emerald and blue chandeliers made in 1840 for the Indian market. The pillars which support the roof are surmounted by varnished palm fronds. 'My own touch that,' he says. 'Perhaps it's as well, really, that Oliver Messel died. There would have been terrible tears about some of my little embellishments.'

As befits the magus of Mustique, Tennant's palace is the most exotic on the island. Among the other houses there is none of the offensive display of grandeur one might expect from a spot so densely enforested with family trees and celebrities. (Just left — the Pembrokes, the Lichfields, the Buckhursts and John Stefanidis. Just arrived — the Duke and Duchess of Kent, Princess Margaret, Roddy Llewellyn and Lord and Lady Hesketh. Permanent fixtures — Brian Alexander, Viscountess Royston. Settling in — Mick Jagger. Banned — Steve Rubell. 'I was for him, actually,' said Tennant. 'But the others objected. Personally I'm happy to welcome anyone who's desperate to get here.')

The tempo and demeanour of Mustique is almost Tennant's single highest achievement. All the people who work for him are distinguished by their cordial directness — Brian Alexander, a tolerant blond Adonis who manages Mustique after a spell on the marketing side of the Rank organisation; Nevill Turner, a droll ex-Guards officer with a boisterous wife who now has his own successful development and restaurant, Dolittle's, on St Lucia from where he acts as Tennant's agent, and the wise and genial John Golds, a director of the Mustique company and chairman of eighteen others in the Caribbean and British Guyana, who provides an endless supply of road doctors and sand experts. Tennant himself slyly attributes the low-key sociability of Mustique to the influence of Princess Margaret. 'She's always behaved impeccably here and it's kept us on our toes,' but anyone who's tasted Tennant's grilled coconut in his bamboo dining-room tinkling with Filipino shells knows it's old smoothie who's responsible.

Colin Tennant landed on the white beach of Endeavour Bay, Mustique, in 1959, an island only three miles long and one and a half miles wide, with a population of 150. He sold the family's tea plantation in Trinidad for £44,500 and bought Mustique from two Irish spinsters called the Misses Hazell for £45,000. His friends wondered what he thought he was playing at, buying a bankrupt plantation, but at the time Tennant had nothing better to do. He had been forced out of the City by his father selling up the family firm when he was only 38, leaving him with no job and a great deal of money. In any case, he believed from the start that Mustique could be made viable.

'Tourism,' he explains, 'after the war was the setting up of large hotels — white reserves, imposed from the outside. They thought people wanted cocktails and cha-cha-cha beside the pool, waited on hand and foot by grinning Negro servants. When I came here in 1959 I tried to set about building from the inside outwards and events have proved I was ahead of my time. In Antigua, where the villagers were ignored by the tourists, the people have turned against whites. The villagers in Mustique enjoy the same confidence they used to enjoy in Scotland. I have been able to employ most of them, when before there was no work at all, and those too old to employ I've given pensions, which has helped them to retain their status in the village. Almost more important, they are protected by my standards of behaviour. No one would dream of insulting a waiter or the girl who works in the shop because I'd chase them off the island. I don't hesitate to behave disgracefully if I feel my territory is being violated. If I see a tourist dropping waste paper I'll rub it in his face. When I saw someone shooting fish on the reef I jumped out of the car and seized his spear gun.'

In 1960, Tennant gave a plot of Mustique to Princess Margaret as a wedding present. Gradually, as he started to develop the island, he returned less and less to Glen, his 300-roomed house in Scotland, and saw 'all too little' of his wife and four children.

He discovered in himself a passion for the Caribbean. 'I do have,' he says, 'an affinity with black people. Not to the extent of my cousin, Francis Wyndham, who actually wants to *be* a black person, nor, I hope, in a spirit of guilt and condescension. I learnt at Oxford the importance of being oneself at all times. I *am* the Honourable Colin Tennant or as I used to say to my nanny when I was five, "I

Opposite. Out to lunch: *Brian A., Princess M., Colin T., Reinaldo H., Tina B., Signor X. and Carolina H. picnicking under the trees.* Over the top: *Colin T. under the palm-tree pillars of his Oliver Messel drawing-room*

am the horrible Colin Tennant, and there's nothing I can do about that".'

He had an early taste of exotic travel in his school holidays. These he spent with his mother to whom he was warded when his parents were divorced. 'We always went to remote places because they were cheaper. We were also inspired by the example of my grandmother Lady Muriel Paget who was a great traveller and heroine in the Lady Hester Stanhope idiom. She spent ten years in Russia reorganising the English community and the attic of her house in the West Country was always stuffed with fugitive governesses. People think of me as a bit eccentric now, but in my grandparents' day people were almost expected to be eccentric. My grandfather was an amateur scientist who wanted to stamp out speech. At meals we never spoke. He encouraged us to sing madrigals instead. It's where I got my passion for songs, particularly music-hall numbers of the 1880s, which I'll perform at the drop of *any* hat. What a splendid man my grandfather was — he would whistle and hum at the same time.'

Travel also seemed to Tennant a way of liberating himself from the rigidities of class. Oxford, where he won a scholarship to read history, seemed something of a disappointment for this reason. 'I thought I was going to be like a Yank at Oxford, getting terribly chummy with all sorts of people. I found one was limited to the people one already knew. I succumbed to my social abilities and was always in London having lunch at embassies or going to Paris for dinner. Sir Ian Gilmour's about the only one of my Oxford friends I still see.'

It was only with Mustique that Tennant really felt he could combine these 'social abilities' with a certain manic creative drive. He built roads, planted coconut groves, moved the village to a better site, flew in building labour from the parent island of St Vincent. At the suggestion of Princess Margaret, because he was Lord Snowdon's uncle, Tennant invited Oliver Messel to design the earliest houses and fashion the only hotel, the Cotton House, out of an old warehouse which Tennant then furnished with antique tea chests, biscuit tins and bamboo furniture and opened up for business. He sold it two years ago to a French Hotelier, Guy de la Houssaye, who used to run the Bakoua in Martinique. Today a four-acre plot of land in Mustique costs £40,000. With 40 houses already built, there are only 52 more plots to sell. The peace and privacy of the island has been protected not simply by Tennant's taste but Tennant's law — he decreed that each house must stand in an average of four acres.

Apart from the nineteen-roomed Cotton House Hotel, Basil's Beach Bar is the only rallying point on Mustique, a bamboo stockade slung over the rushing water of a coral reef where Lord Hesketh's yacht had just put in when I arrived. Basil himself is a convivial native of St Vincent who was rescued from a motor-cycle accident by one of Tennant's partners and spent a year in hospital before he could get across to Mustique to say thank you. He has stayed on ever since. The success of his bar was confirmed when Lord Royston's merry widow, Virginia, came to Mustique for a holiday and fell into the arms of Basil with whom, they say, she is as happy as the night is long. A taste for philosophy dominates the decor at Basil's. One pensée over the bar reads, 'Am I a mushroom? They keep me in the dark and feed me lots of bullshit.'

It is here, at half past eight when the running buffet of suckling pig, lobster, yams, breadfruit and heart of palm is just about ready to be served that the royal party arrives. I realise something is happening when Lady Cassel's party start going down like nine-pins and Colin Tennant, waving a silver topped walking-stick, deftly parts the queue to the spit. Into the gap step a bronzed and beaming Duke and Duchess of Kent, Princess Margaret, Roddy Llewellyn, and the Princess's house guests, the Venezuelan jet setters Carolina and Reinaldo Herrera. At first it appears that Señora Herrera — an Evita beauty who constantly crops up on the world's best-dressed women list, is accompanied by a giant sting-ray, but on closer observation it turns out to be an outsize taffeta bow that forms the bodice of her dress. The royals take their seats at one of the 30 tables ranged round the dance floor to face a makeshift stage. Tennant, meanwhile, refuses to sit down at all. His self-possession is giving way by stages to a mood of nervous euphoria until he leaps onto the stage in a white track suit and blue Afro wig and prances barefoot among the puddles of a tropical cloudburst leading the audience, a mixed bag of American yacht hands, Mustique blacks, a US rugby champion, a posse of civil engineers flown in by John Golds and a smattering of peers, in 'Happy days are here again'.

'Mustique,' comments an amazed blonde at the next table, 'is a very expensive way for Colin to work out his schizophrenia.' But before he can work it out any further, Act One has emerged from behind the sheet that serves as a backcloth — The Amazing Dancing Dwarf, made up of Mustique's master builder and Nevill Turner in a

Rosie Boot's Guide to London Bachelors

Nicholas de Rothschild

Last orders now for Nicholas de Rothschild. I can't recommend his week (video, Chinese food, Fulham) but his weekends are definitely a cut above his peers. The chauffeur parks his Porsche and the housekeeper does his shopping. And we're not talking now about some clapped-out family pile stuffed with garrulous relations. No, Lower Exbury House is a deliciously comfy five-bedroomed cottage in the grounds of the Rothschild estate near Southampton, overlooking the River Beaulieu. In other words, it'll take more than the lure of creature comforts to make him settle down.

Rothschild, nearly 30, has looked progressively more like the young Edward VII since he began to lose his hair. Actually, the Hunnish beard is a distinct improvement, lending him a soigné Clement Freud air that goes well with his surname. The elegant new image is matched by his refurbished terraced house in Fulham. The sitting-room, anyway, has distinctly improved since the days when his piranha fish kept eating each other and his flat-mate, Julian Summer, jumped on a shopping-bag full of Justin de Blank avocado mousse. Now he shares the house with *Not the Nine O'Clock News* producer John Lloyd and an advertising chap called Julian Thomas. No problems here.

His taste in women seems refreshingly straightforward, i.e. available and not chubby. He is said, however, to have some difficulty in concentration. The 'actually I was going out with two girls, now I'm going out with neither' syndrome has caused him to be sighted dining tout seul sometimes at the Ho Lee Fook.

The main worry with Nick might be in persuading him not to blow the family fortune on investments in the unsavoury world of light entertainment. At Harrow and Cambridge he had seemed safe enough from such influences, reading anthropology and archaeology and enjoying bibulous evenings at the Pitt Club.

But these days his video company, The Electronic Picture House, has a disturbingly business-like air. He talks with alarming pride of *The Glittering Crowns*, an historical video documentary about the crowned heads of Europe he pushed out to coincide with the Royal Wedding. True, he'd expect you to mug up on photographing butterflies, and not to look crumpled when travelling with him and his father, Edmund de Rothschild, to lesser-known parts of Guinea, but showbiz has got him. One senses an embryonic longing to be not a Rothschild but a Grade. Will the banking barony soon be associated with a new form of Muppets? I'm sure a soothing talk with Miss Piggy would bring him to his senses. Hollywood is much less fun than the River Beaulieu, but take your tap shoes to Lower Exbury just in case.

false moustache. Then, after a hectic warm-up from Tennant, his blue eyes flashing under his wig, Act Two is announced. There is a small hiccup: the organist has to be persuaded he will not be electrocuted by the damp if he strikes a chord. Tennant is still working on him when the artists appear — two fuzzy-wigged, sequin-spectacled crooners flanking a stately soloist in a purple tent dress. It is HRH Princess Margaret with Roddy Llewellyn and Reinaldo Herrera. A fascinated silence ensues and the Kents corpse as the trio belt out a resounding rendition of 'Chatanooga Choo Choo'. They bow to a storm of applause and the whole of Basil's swarms onto the dance floor. Tennant, in his element now, plunges off into the crowd bearing the Afro wig which he claps on the head of anyone looking too sober or respectable. 'There's no one this wig can't improve,' he cries, cramming it over the eyes of a bespectacled old boy engaged in a perilous twist. Princess Margaret hits the floor with Roddy for a majestic rock and roll, surrounded now by the wild boogy of long-legged Lady Hesketh partnering three of Basil's more ebullient waiters.

The next day at a small lunch party Tennant throws for Princess Margaret she is still worrying about her performance. 'Would you have believed,' she mourned, 'we had all been rehearsing from three o'clock in the afternoon.'

'It was the organist who let you down, Ma'am,' says Tennant, restored to his usual elegance. 'He was suddenly unable to strike a G. Anyway, I've made enquiries this morning and the general feeling here is that you were much better than you thought.'

Tennant's behaviour at this lunch and subsequently makes one see that however close he'd sailed to the wind of impropriety the night before he was never in danger of losing control. The ever-present possibility that he might do so, however, creates a tension between himself and Princess Margaret that seems to fulfil a mutual need. His subtle understanding of the constraints on royalty makes it possible for the Princess to enjoy the illusion of escaping them without ever being, as Tennant puts it, 'declassed', while *her* strict imposition of limits to informality stops him going over the top.

Tennant can only get away with bending the rules because he knows them so well. He handles the tension perfectly and is amused rather than discomfited when, on another day in the middle of an alfresco picnic at Macaroni beach, the Princess suddenly pulls rank, with the cry, 'What, no mustard! How am I expected to eat sausages without mustard!' and the whole party leaps to its feet in consternation. Isn't it a strain? I ask him.

'Of course it is,' he replies, breezily. 'The more so, because it can't look like one. The only time things have ever gone wrong here was the time I left the island for a week and Roddy's ulcer burst and the Princess was left alone here which was intolerable for her. I have to think all the time of what it must be like to be her or indeed anyone who comes here — and anticipate needs without being obtrusive. It's a very small place, so I have to stagger the thrills. I waited a week, for instance, before giving the Kents lobsters. It may look like frivolity but making these visits a success takes constant imagination — one quality I must say I've always possessed. It's why I was so good at finding plovers' eggs when I was a boy. I could always think myself into the mind of the plover and know just where she'd lay her eggs.'

Tennant, of course, is highly qualified to run a Club Mediterranée for royalty. He comes from a family of equerries and his wife, Lady Anne, is lady-in-waiting to Princess Margaret. His relationship with his wife seems to thrive on the same tension as his relationship with her boss. Lady Anne is, by all accounts, a stickler for correct form and dislikes what she regards as the departures from it in their informalities of Mustique. 'She's amazingly grand,' a friend said. 'She insists on the highest social standards. She even had her tiara remodelled for the Wilton Ball.'

Lady Anne only visits Mustique once a year at Easter with their nine-year-old twin daughters and she has refused to have their eldest son, Charlie, home since he became a heroin addict at the age of sixteen. Their youngest son, Henry, nineteen, is down to study tropical agriculture at Trinidad university and is currently living in a small hotel at St Lucia doing Maths O-level and Transcendental Meditation. One feels that Tennant has a very soft spot for his unconventional boys, particularly the erring Charlie. 'Charlie is,' he says, 'in spite of it all, such a star, such a charmer. I'm afraid he was the casualty of the rather different social attitudes of my wife and I. She saw him as a naughty boy who should be spanked. I saw him as an unhappy boy who should be psychoanalysed. I took him away from public school against her inclination and sent him to a progressive place. I'm sure now I was wrong. She's brought up the twins her own way, and I must say they're perfect, always busy, never bored. If they're not sewing, they're playing hopscotch, if they're not playing hopscotch they're making those potato things. I suppose it's much healthier than Charlie's experiments or Henry's Transcendental Meditation. The trouble is, I could never find it in my heart to condemn Charlie. I know that if that sort of badness had been available to me when I was younger I would have jumped at it as well. In my own youth one just didn't have to go that far to create an effect. I remember causing outrage for weeks by getting my tailor to make me a suit with no pockets.'

Now Tennant is beginning to tire of playing Prospero. Two years ago he had to sell out his majority share of Mustique but was asked back to be chairman when things began, as he predicted, to slip and go wrong. In the interim he flirted with being a Scottish Nationalist MP, but eventually abandoned it. He is still a passionate Scottish Nationalist. 'The trouble was, Scotland couldn't take a Nationalist with an Etonian accent seriously and it seemed counter-productive to have one's views noticed purely because one seems so eccentric for holding them. Also it became rather tricky to persist in advocating policies which were obviously deeply repugnant to the Queen.'

He feels too young to retire on Mustique yet, but is in a dilemma about what to do. 'I suspect,' he says, 'my life-long smokescreen of frivolity has turned me in the eyes of London into a lotus-eater' — an absurdity to anyone who has seen Tennant's fastidious energy moving mountains on Mustique. He blames himself. 'I used to have,' he reflects, 'a great tendency to seduce people. I knew I could "get" them and I'd waste my time showing them I could. Now I'm beginning to feel being shocking is not very fruitful. People look and then pass on. Sometimes,' he adds with a particularly vivid smile, 'I think the only person I've shocked irreparably is my wife and the only person who has been seduced is me.'

THERE IS NOTHING LIKE A THANE

(of Cawdor)

The best way to see Scotland is to take the train to Edinburgh, hire a clapped-out Cortina and a clan chieftain's son to drive it. With this basic equipment, you can dial your way through *Debrett's*, soliciting beds for the night in historic houses. Such was my reasoning, anyway, when I asked a civil young man from Perth to chauffeur me on a three-day tour of the Scottish gratin that would start in the Borders with the Binnings of Mellerstain and the Maxwell Stuarts of Ancient Traquair, go West to Ayrshire to visit the famous wag, the Hon Robert Corbett, take in the Telfer Smolletts on the Banks of Loch Lomond and finally drop us well and truly North of the Border with the Thane of Cawdor. Did he think he could manage this? 'No prob,' said the clan chieftain's son. We reverse along George Street and speed out of Edinburgh, basking in a rare heat wave, towards Gordon.

The Beautiful Binnings

Mellerstain is the border home of Lord Binning, reformed-hippie heir to the Earl of Haddington. It is not, as the clan chieftain's son described, 'quite a pretty house with some very nice views' but a socking great stately home built by Robert Adam in 1770. It is sunset when we roll up and, emptied of tourists, the house is poised reflectively at the end of a long drive, exuding Augustan taste and order. Lady Binning is in the kitchen, making a salad. She is a ravishing blonde of 27, but in her lemon boiler suit and bare feet she doesn't look a day over sixten.

'I can't think what's happening to Binning,' she says. 'We've been to a wedding and had far too much Pimms.' She takes us out for a drink to a large, enclosed courtyard, part of the stables which have now been turned into their living quarters and converted into a spacious, unpretentious home. Here, plastic deck-chairs and a tangle of sunday papers are the relics of the Binnings' weekend. 'Binning wants to put a pond out here,' she tells me, 'so he can photograph his filthy frogs.'

Lord Binning, it transpires, is an enthusiastic photographer. His speciality is pornographic nature studies of tree trunks that look like loins, and close-ups of double-decker toads. At 38, he wears smoked John Lennon glasses and carries about with him an air of laid-back gloom which only clears at dinner when the clan chieftain's son asks for 'another hit of lettuce'.

He has been living permanently at Mellerstain since his marriage five years ago to Prue Rutherford Hayles. The rural conversion seems to be complete although hints of a past life surface in his obsessive reading of *Chopper*, the magazine for motorbike buffs. He rarely comes to London and his holiday this year will be a fishing expedition to Orkney. 'I'll take my wee tent,' he says, 'and fish in the sea. It's free and I don't have to book.' The following weekend's social diary held a hunt ball on Saturday, a raft race on Sunday at which the Binnings were to be the judges, and an afternoon watching the horse-driving at nearby Floors Castle, home of the Duke and Duchess of Roxburghe. 'If we want to catch a film we can always go to the local flea-pit in Kelso,' he says. 'Unless it happens to be Tuesday, when, of course, it's bingo.'

Although the Binnings live at Mellerstain, the family seat is Tyninghame, a red, turreted, Gothic mansion overlooking the sea on the west coast of Scotland. Lord Binning's parents, the Earl (now 85) and Countess of Haddington have lived here since 1952, returning to Mellerstain in the winter to hunt. The whole family moves to Mellerstain at Christmas when the main house is opened up for ten days. 'It's wonderful to see wellies and coats outside rooms which spend the year looking perfect,' says Prue. 18,000 tourists a year visit the house. The Binnings would like 25,000 but, apart from vintage car rallies and horse-driving heats in which Prince Philip takes part, they make no strenuous play for the public.

'It's funny,' says Prue Binning as we wander round the lake at the bottom of the garden and look back at the perfect green terraces, 'to think here one is, for life as it were, unable to change the scenery like other people even if one wanted. At first I worried about moving any of the plants. There were some salmony roses at the front that really *weren't* amazing, but I didn't dare move them because they were put in by my ma-in-law who is a famously clever gardener. But then I discussed it with her and she said, "Of course you must move them. They look absolutely disgusting." I felt so relieved . . .'

'We must get a decent billiards table,' Lord Binning says. 'It's nice to have a good game when you come in from stalking.' He stays up late after dinner with the clan chieftain's son, talking about 'old times'. It clearly rejuvenates him, for the next morning he puts on a cowboy hat and a small red spotted kerchief and suggests we all drive to Traquair.

The Modernised Maxwell Stuarts

Traquair, a careworn fortress overlooking the River Tweed, is the oldest inhabited house in Scotland. It is traditionally the home of lost causes. Its 1st laird took the wrong side in the Civil War and ended his days on his uppers in the streets of Edinburgh. Its 5th laird supported Bonnie Prince Charlie. Peter and Flora Maxwell Stuart, the 20th laird and his wife, are a dedicated pair, determined to keep Traquair in the family. Until ten years ago they had no electric light. A fortune has been spent saving the house from the neglect rendered by a succession of sporting bachelor uncles who revelled in its freezing authenticity and never threw anything away except the family jewels. When the Binnings' red Porsche flashes up the two-mile drive (no lost causes in *their* history) Flora Maxwell Stuart is busting a gut preparing a needlework exhibition and her husband is watching out in eager dread for a busload of visiting Italians.

'Quick, we'll rush ahead and see the house before them,' he cries and we bolt up to the library, stuffed with handwritten letters from Stuart kings, then on to the bedroom where Mary Queen of Scots slept and down to the brew house where the still makes 25,000 bottles a year of Traquair House Ale. 'Traquair,' he pants, 'has played host in its time to 27 kings.'

We adjourn to a high-walled patio leading out from a worn, comfortable sitting-room where the Binnings and a party of family guests are knocking back the ale. Mr Maxwell Stuart's nephew, a serious young man in enormous shorts, hands round quiche Lorraine while his aunt describes the happy change in her life wrought by a toasted-sandwich machine. A peacock screams. 'The good thing about that peacock,' Mr Maxwell Stuart muses, 'is that it gets around so much people think there's more than one of him.' Is there a ghost at Traquair? I ask. 'I wish there was,' says his wife with a harassed smile. 'Ghosts *do* bring in the public.'

Bobby Corbett's Crash Pad

Humming with the house ale we hit the road westwards for Ayrshire; a straight route of motorways and heather. 'Know anybody in Glasgow we could call on for tea?' I ask the clan chieftain's son. 'Only Jimmy Boyle in Barlinnie jail,' he says and we hurtle on through biscuit-coloured Stewarton in search of Cankerton, the home of the Hon Robert Corbett. It finally materialises behind a clump of trees, a small, low-slung farmhouse surrounded by waving fields. Corbett, now 39 and joint master of the fox hounds, has lived here for three years perfecting his brilliant comic prose since the day when Rowallan Castle passed to his nephew. He opens the door, an insouciant wasp with a thickening girth, wearing his shirt sleeves. With him is a house guest, Mr Rick Parker Bowles, an ageing Hooray Henry with a huge glistening chin and severe indigestion. It is soon evident that the two men are at the end of a lost weekend. 'New faces, thank God,' barks Corbett. 'Parker Bowles is driving me quite mad. He never gets up and he never goes to bed. The telephone went at two o'clock this afternoon and it was his *alarm* call!'

'How was old Binning?' asks Parker Bowles. 'Last time I saw him he was in a restaurant in London, ordering a grilled stoat.' This is the tenth day of what was intended by Parker Bowles as an overnight visit. He arrived to collect his car and drive it back to London, but wrote it off trying to dodge a cat and now is returning south on the sleeper with Corbett in time to catch the Chelsea Flower Show.

Inside, the house has the temporary air of the confirmed bachelor

— there are single beds and electric fires and clusters of photographs of the late Lord Rowallan looking forbidding and the Hon Robert buttoned up in his hunting kit in a sea of hounds. The castle was nearly his or so everyone believed when his elder brother Arthur Corbett married in 1963 for the second time to April Ashley, formerly able seaman George Jamieson. Hearing of the engagement Robert sent a telegram to his brother which read 'Congratulations. Can I be bridesmaid.' Today Arthur Corbett runs a bar in Marbella and sports very long fingernails and a succession of hirsute beauties. Legend has it that one evening, when he descended to dinner at Rowallan Castle wearing a dress, the butler turned to the late Lord Rowallan and murmured, 'It's not what I laid out, my lord.' 'It's hardly surprising about Arthur,' says Bobbie after a meal of Vichyssoise and Marks and Spencer lasagne. 'Daddy was such a puritan he'd have to react against him. Dinner was served at 7.15 preceded by a *teeny* glass of sherry that was whipped round so quickly the butler had virtually to wear running shoes. Now, if you'll excuse me, I have to go and pack for the season. Do sharpen,

Parker Bowles, or we'll miss the train.'

'I'll just finish this porter,' yawns Parker Bowles, 'and I'm yours, I'm yours!' The two men rattle off in a taxi at half past ten, leaving me alone with the snapshots and the clan chieftain's son who gets very Scottish after his sixth glass of port.

Going Public with the Telfer Smoletts

We speed northwards towards Inverness the next morning, stopping only in Glasgow to have lunch at the Ubiquitous Chip with Roddy Martine, the lanky editor of the *Scottish Field*. He tells me that Glasgow is the most swinging place in the British Isles, citing as evidence a gay 2001 party and a new coffee bar. The weather has broken as we leave Glasgow for Loch Lomond and a mist stokes down the blazing greens and golds, turning everything to dun. It is wilder, woodier and more mountainous as we approach the loch. By the time we reach Cameron House, the mini château of the Telfer Smolletts, the military-minded descendants of the eighteenth-century novelist, it is bucketing down. Even so, Mr Telfer Smollett is waiting at the pay booth to give us a guided tour of the bear park, spouting tourist figures all the while and vaulting in and out of monkey cages. Large notices explain, 'This is not a stately home. It is a *family* home.'

The Telfer Smolletts themselves live on a self-contained floor of the house. 'People come here to see how the other half live, not to see Rembrandts,' says Mrs Telfer Smollett, a composed blonde, and indeed even as we talk there is an aroma of the lamb chops the other half had for lunch. The grounds of Cameron House, twenty acres of wildlife reserve and woodland are let out for pop concerts. 'It was highly successful last year,' says Mr Telfer Smollett. 'Does the Boomtown Mice mean anything to you? Or Tizzy Lizzy? Yup, they came and it was a sell-out.' Running the bear park alone must be a considerable expense. Do they have grants? 'No grants, none,' he says. 'We're very much a private enterprise but we don't regret for a minute the decision to go public.'

'No shit,' whistles the clan chieftain's son and we bowl off north towards the 'temple-haunting martlet' — the climax of our highland fling.

This Castle Hath a Pleasant Seat

It is dusk as we speed through the broom-splashed hedgerows of the Cawdor estate to check out the thane. The castle is gratifyingly rugged after the Augustan seemliness of Mellerstain and the toffee-nosed turrets of Cameron House. It is a honey-coloured shortbread fortress set in 50,000 acres of rustling woods and lonely moors. The thane and thaness emerge as we cross the drawbridge looking as if they'd been chosen for their parts by Central Casting. At 48 he has the morose good looks of Richard Burton before the booze and she, his second wife, is a tall, dramatic redhead dressed like a Jacobean princeling in skin-tight black pants and a black velvet tunic. They don't seen to go a bundle over the clan chieftain's son.

I am led up a side staircase and down a long, tartan-carpeted corridor freshly done up in Dulux Siesta. This is where the family sleep during the summer when the castle is open to the public. Guests are provided with a key to the corridor and requested to lock themselves in and out. 'Otherwise,' Lord Cawdor says, 'you might find someone from Huddersfield in your bed trying to put a date to your pyjamas.' Lady Cawdor explains in detail how to find the library in the tower after I have changed for dinner but half an hour later I am still roaming the tartan corridor shaking my gory locks like Banquo's ghost in search of a landmark.

Lord Cawdor's 22-year-old daughter, Lady Emma Campbell, is dispatched to collect me. In her long black cheesecloth nightshirt over drainpipe jeans she is straight out of a Charles Addams cartoon. 'Are you waiting like a nervous bride?' she asks languidly and teeters off ahead of me on stiletto clogs through a cordoned-off sitting-room and up a twisting stone staircase. This is a rare, recuperative visit home for Emma. In London she has a very trendy time, saying 'No swert' a lot and sharing a flat near the Fulham Road ABC with her sister Lady Liza, twenty, who recently made her modelling debut as the heroine in a true-love trash magazine. The boys, Colin (eighteen), Frederick (fifteen), and the youngest girl Laura (thirteen) are still at school.

In the library the thane and thaness are sitting in worn tartan armchairs enjoying a drink against the wailing background of Leonard Cohen. It is a large, cosy room bulging with second-hand books which Lord Cawdor buys at sales. The walls are adorned with a charcoal mural of the Macbeth witches drawn by Lady Kensington in the nineteenth century. The Macbeth myth swirls about the castle quite erroneously. Shakespeare was about 300 years out in his choice of Cawdor as the venue for the action of the play, but later Cawdors seem to have enjoyed this addition to their history. When the castle opened to the public five years ago Shakespeare's plot did a lot to aid what the present thane describes as 'the pleasing patter of pound notes'.

'King Duncan didn't die in this room as the Victorian Cawdors said,' he says. 'He died in a skirmish outside Elgin. Duncan was killed in 1040. They knew this room was fourtenth century so it was just a black lie. They invested in a Victorian oak bed which wasn't a week older than 1840 and swore Duncan had died in it. It so infuriated my father he had it thrown out of the window.'

Dinner is Scotch salmon served by candlelight in a small oval dining-room. We help ourselves from the sideboard. Breakfast is at

10 a.m. in the same room with little conversation except for Lord Cawdor's comments as he opens his post. 'Ha! That's rich! An invitation from My Lord Seafield to shoot on the 14th of November.' One face missing at breakfast is the clan chieftain's son. His charm had finally bombed at midnight, and he was shown the drawbridge.

Hugh Cawdor is the 6th Earl and 24th Thane — 'At least, I think I am. Perhaps I should go and look it up in case I've gone up, like a point on the Stock Exchange.' He went to Eton and Oxford, reading PPE then zoology and agriculture at Magdalen College. He was advised to leave after one year on the grounds of indolence and went to Cirencester where he won the prize for practical forestry. He remains an impressive tree buff to this day, able to date and categorise the most obscure species on his estate and name the botanist who discovered it. He gained practical farming experience after Cirencester, running his father's estates in Wales. These had passed into the family in 1689 when the thane of the time married, in Cawdor's words, 'the right tart'. In fact, the family house, Stackpole, had been torn down and rebuilt in neo-Georgian style in the neighbouring country of Carmarthenshire. 'It looked,' says Lord Cawdor wistfully, 'like Sunningdale Police Station.' They lived here until his father died in 1970 and the Welsh lands were sold off to pay the death duties. 'It was very sad,' Emma recalls. 'Like chopping a portrait in half.'

'Oh, I don't know,' her father says, 'I think it's quite a cosy feeling that it's gone to the Electricity Generating Board's Pension Fund.'

On his father's death Lord Cawdor moved permanently to Scotland and set about opening the castle to the public. 'I put in a pitch-and-curse course and had a few tutorials with Edward Montagu at Beaulieu but that's about all. It's been quite a success really, considering there are no *Mona Lisas*.'

In fact, its success is largely due to the pervading wit of the 24th thane. Hugh Cawdor is one of those talented dilettantes thrown up from time to time in the British aristocracy and appreciated, like a banned work of art, by an amused circle of lucky friends. His room notes to the castle are a delicious mixture of erudition and satire guaranteed equally to delight the expert or the philistine. 'The large oak cabinet conceals a television set,' read his notes for the Blue Room, 'and above the door is a cartoon in oils by Henry Bunbury of the artist and the 1st Lord Cawdor as peasants. The cream-coloured perforated plates are Staffordshire salt-glaze. Mind your heads unless you are a Papuan pygmy.'

The notes are such a pleasure after the dry impersonality of National Trust guide books, that other stately-home owners want him to come and write their brochures. 'The Duke of Argyll keeps asking me to come and do his,' he tells me, 'but I told him that it's all right for me to take the piss out of my own house, but I can hardly do it to his. Anyway, dukes have got to be a bit ducal haven't they? Otherwise, what's the point of them?'

Last year, 45,000 people came to Cawdor, so many that in future summers the family are moving to a large Georgian farmhouse in the grounds. Every September they move anyway to Drynachen, a Victorian shooting-lodge high on the moors. 'It's very very simple,' Lady Cawdor tells me. 'It sleeps 28 and just has the basics.'

It is, in fact, a grey rabbit-warren of a house with enormous old-fashioned baths, and pasted over every doorway there is a flight of paper grouse stuck up by Lord Cawdor for guests to practise their aim. While the men shoot, the women stay at home and prepare the lunch or amuse themselves. How do they amuse themselves? I ask, surveying from the window an infinity of heather. 'There's masses to do,' Lady Cawdor says firmly. 'One can look for wild mushrooms, for a start.' Looking for wild mushrooms is a change of pace from her urban life before she maried three years ago. Born a Czecho-slavakian countess, she spent fourteen years in Paris building up a highly successful public relations firm with accounts which included American Express and the Canadian government. 'My friends in Paris ask me how I can come to a castle in the wilds of Scotland and not miss my career,' she says. 'My answer is *with no trouble at all.* The people are so solid and strong. They care about the family so much I now feel I belong here. We never go to London for more than 24 hours. It would be terrible, for instance, to miss the cherry blossom.'

'Or indeed the plane back to London,' says Lord Cawdor genially. He waves me off at Inverness airport, wearing his kilt, a timeless self-possessed figure amongst the sea of bustling business suits.

BLUE SERGE

Gainsbourg gets the wind up

Serge Gainsbourg always went out of his way to look like the before picture in a cosmetic surgeon's waiting-room. Now, at 52, he no longer has to try. He is a human ash-tray with duvet-sized bags beneath his hallucinogenic blue eyes and his gentian chin shows definite tufts of grey. After ten years of living with the English actress Jane Birkin he still talks like a Bohemian Inspector Clouseau.

'Jane left me for a yoong film director,' he told me sorrowfully when he was last in London to promote his first novel and a reggae LP. 'She walked out on July the 13th. The next day it was the feu d'artifice in my head. I was blind. I cried for three months. You cannot believe a man of 52 cry so merch as me. Now I am alone in a beautiful house in Saint Germain. No child. No cat. No fiancée. My derg is dead. I wait for the sun to go down and drop real tears into my champagne.'

In France, Serge Gainsbourg is something of a cult figure ('a marginal,' he demurs). He was known first as a painter, then as a night-club singer who drew fashionable crowds and intellectual reviews, and more lately as a screenwriter and novelist. Here and in America he is hardly known at all. 'I went to sign copies of my book in Sharring Cross Road and it was a *flope*,' he told me. 'There was no one there except a yoong girl who asked me how much was the price of a poster.' What celebrity he does enjoy here stems from a record he made in 1969 with Jane Birkin, an orgasmic recitative backed by a melodic electric organ. It was an interminable number one, largely due to the BBC's attempts to ban it and the mythology amongst English girls that Frenchmen make better lovers. In America, it stopped in the charts, appropriately enough, at 69.

'Je t'aime' cast Gainsbourg in his most unlikely role of all, international heart-throb. Today the only relic of his seducer's charm is an infectious nicotine cackle that suggests amazement that anyone should go on taking him seriously. He describes his career as an 'attention to surprise'. 'I stop painting because in my painting I put my soul,' he says, 'and I don't want to sell my soul. My songs are rerbish. I started singing when I was 30 in a little night-club and people come and say — what great songs this ugly guy sings. I was very famous but I had no merney. Then come along the little girls

Rosie Boot's Guide to London Bachelors

Adam Shand Kydd

If you're still looking for an upmarket surname you couldn't do better than Adam Shand Kydd. Its tangential aroma of the Princess of Wales goes down a treat with bank-managers and American Express and he doesn't spend *that* much time on the famed sheep-farm on the Isle of Mull.

Adam, 27, is the son of wall-paper tycoon Peter Shand Kydd and his first wife, Janet, who now lives in Suffolk. He has tall, sloppy good looks and a ferociously laid-back air that repels the uncool admirer. He was educated at Stowe, where what friends describe as a 'mixed ride' became less mixed when he drove a Mini into the school chapel. After a precipitate departure he did a stint at Davis's tutorial and then moved on to work at the Portobello Hotel in Stanley Gardens, where the bar is open all night and fringe rock stars can have sandwiches served by an equally laid-back staff at 4 a.m. Adam, it seems, was not known for his politeness and is remembered for his famous 'Madam, if you think the coffee was bad, wait till you taste the hamburger.' Nonetheless, his Burne-Jones languor has gained him some classy female attention in the shape of such Mayfair Mata Haris as Angela Gorgas, Lucretia Stewart and Carinthia West.

Since the Portobello days Adam has dabbled at being a publisher's reader, although no publisher he's worked for seems to be prepared to admit it. After a spell with the first Elephant Man, David Schofield, as a flatmate, he now lives alone in a spiral-staircased flat in Arundel Gardens, mixing with the Ladbroke Grove beau monde and Guinness/Rothschild circles. So what's the point in pursuing shambolic Shand Kydd? Well, just think who might be with you on the McBrain's ferry.

and boys playing rerk music, I was suddenly too old. So I do 'Je t'aime' which is very shocking, very sexy and make me very rich. Today the little boys and girls are 35 and too old, but I made myself yoong again because I do a reggae record in Jamaica, *Aux armes etcetera*, which all the yoong peoples love. Now, I have just acted in a film with Catherine Deneuve and all the press say I am her lerver. Gainsbourg is always making waves.'

Controversy hyped his reggae record just as it had 'Je t'aime'. One of the tracks is a reggae version of the Marseillaise. *Le Figaro* wrote a furious leader denouncing Gainsbourg, by birth a Russian Jew, for ridiculing the national anthem by setting it to a black rhythm. 'Can you believe that?' snickers Gainsbourg. 'France is so right wing it's incroyable. They bomb synagogues. It's like a flashback. Where can you go now to have any fern? Paris is the peets. Since Jean-Paul Sartre, nothing happen. Even fashion is still Saint Laurent. Who is it for? The Arabs? The Rothschilds? But England, I think, is down, too. I miss Mr Heath. He made me laugh so much, that man, his face, his boats, the way his shoulders go up and down. I miss the beautiful girls.' He scans the menu and paddles sadly in his Eurasian girlfriend's neck. She is a twenty-year-old model who has to be anonymous, because 'she belongs to anozzer man'.

'What shall I eat, Serge?' she asks. 'Black pooding,' he replies which amuses him so much he coughs for ten minutes into his Pernod.

Gainsbourg's novel, *Yevgenii Sokolov,* took six years to complete and is 100 pages of very large type. It is the story of a Surrealist painter afflicted by a continuous need to break wind. Ostracised all his life for his complaint, he finally puts it to work when he evolves a painting method which uses his wind to activate his paintbrush. He becomes one of the most celebrated Surrealists in Paris before he finally explodes. In France the book has sold 40,000 copies. This year he and Françoise Sagan will, he says, be the only French authors translated into English.

'All the stuff in my nervel is medically correct,' he tells me proudly. 'Even when he blow up at the end. I had to go to a medical library to look up the details. I said, please, I am Gainsbourg. Let me in. Of course, it is an allegory. My hero is a rascale, a charlatan, pedalling shit, just like the French painters of today. There is a great deal of me in the hero, but distorted like a Francis Bacon painting.'

Gainsbourg owns up to an anal obsession which is confirmed by the hit film he conceived and wrote three years ago also called *Je t'aime*. In it, Jane Birkin, looking exceptionally winning, in a boy's vest, plays a waitress in a roadside café who falls in love with a homosexual truck driver. (Joe Dallessandro). The camera lingers with insistent fascination on her behind which Dallessandro finally cracks in the back of the dustcart. It ends badly when his lover, a histrionic poof with a plastic bag fetish, tries to suffocate her in the bath. In France it is now an underground classic.

How much distortion here? Or are we to assume, since it is its theme tune, that 'Je t'aime . . . moi non plus', the snoggers' anthem from Régines to the Hammersmith Palais, is really a hymn to what Gainsbourg calls 'soodomie'?

He gives the goblin smile of a man who sniffs the possibility of another lucractive controversy. 'My dear girl,' he says slyly, 'Oscar Wilde is nert in prison any more.'

PRIVATE LIFE

Princess Caroline at home in Monaco

When Princess Caroline agreed to appear on the *Tatler* cover we assumed the photographic session would take place in Paris. It was, after all, from their Serene Highnesses' flat in the Avenue Foch that she was most often snapped making reckless sorties into Nescafé society, getting first over-exposed, then divorced, and providing *Paris Match* week in week out with the element of royal glamour they require for their curious editorial admixture of fashion, famine and fame on the skids. But instead we were invited to Monaco.

Here, the Caroline we found was a low-key, serious young woman isolated near the palace in a blush-pink house that is scattered with brainy books and expensive shoes. Her timetable is carefully invigilated by a crisp English secretary who sorts her mail into 'personal', 'official' and 'paranoid'. Her guard-dog, Onyx, lurks in his own room on the ground floor. He has been trained to eat flash-bulbs.

The house is a relatively new acquisition for Princess Caroline. It belonged to her grandfather and became her permanent home after her quickie divorce from Philippe Junot last year. It is close enough to the palace to offer constant protection but far enough away to lead her new, quietly independent life. Habitués of this sat around on the cane furniture breakfasting on Grimaldi croissants while we waited for the princess to descend — a smart young St James's art dealer David Grobb and his wife who had come to help hang the Renoirs in an exhibition mounted by another of her male friends, the elegant Didier Imbert. Full ashtrays, empty bottles of Perrier and creased copies of *The Golden Bowl* suggested earnest up-market fun the night before.

It all seems light years away from the flashy slap and tickle of the blow-dried boulevardier she married. The impression is confirmed when she wanders downstairs wearing jeans and a sweatshirt, a muted tomboy still only 24. One of the most immediately startling things about her is her strong American accent, but on close study her appearance is a sexy jostling of international contradictions. There is a Gallic moodiness in her mouth but a campus casualness in her stride. She manages to be French from the front, American from the back. 'I dread going to Paris these days,' she said. 'Even now I've got Onyx, the paparazzi make it such a hassle. I think of going there to see an exhibition or a movie but then I can't cope with the idea of all those guys hanging around. Fortunately we have a very good musical programme here. Otherwise I read.'

The house is very quiet. It is by no means a mansion but it has, for Monaco, the priceless advantage of a walled garden. It lies behind a secluded entrance. Stairs lead up through peach-coloured archways to her front door. Inside, there is a small, marble-floored hall, a modest dining-room and a light, modern garden room. Her sitting-room which leads off it is an informal mixture of Venetian mirrors, chintz sofas, Moroccan silver and a pair of her grandfather's fanbacked chairs which she has stylishly re-covered in lilac silk. She has keen visual taste. After changing into her own red taffeta Dior wrap for the photo and draping herself expertly over the chair she suddenly broke pose to reposition a vase of flowers. 'Let's not make

Rosie Boot's Guide to London Bachelors

Jasper Guinness

Lord Moyne's grandson, Jasper Guinness, 26, is the greatest heartbreaker of our times. Anne 'Monster' Somerset grieves for him still as do Clarissa Baring and Lady Cosima Vane Tempest Stewart. Rumour has it he was looking pretty relieved at Emma Longman's wedding too and even the dazzling Rachel Ward temporarily lost her cool. Everyone's in love with him.

He's beeen a ladykiller ever since his Oxford days when his free-wheeling cheque book, relaxed (often horizontal) charm and sunny looks made his house the thrumming hub of undergraduate Bohemia. He read law at Christ Church and was a member of the Bullingdon club where he rose to prominence after puking at Kettner's on a club excursion to London.

On graduation, with a third, he found the English winters too much for him and decamped to Florence where he lectures on George Orwell and Evelyn Waugh to impressionable young girls on British Institute courses. In between he hangs out with Harold Acton or lies in bed reading P.G. Wodehouse. Tuscan locals are said to be terrorised by his motorbike.

Every three months or so he comes to London to see his tailor, Vincent's of Savile Row and visit his mother, Mrs Paul Channon. His friends are Bunter Somerset, Timmie Hanbury and all those people who stole the bus outside Annabel's from a Swedish tourist. At night he can be found holding court to a twittering seraglio of posh tearaways at Eleven Park Walk, wearing his familiar uniform of a tiny bow tie and Chianti-flecked white linen trousers. Sometimes, he visits New York where his sister, Catherine, is Andy Warhol's right hand, the only woman allowed access to such gay sanctums as The Anvil and The Toilet. Secretly, however, Jasper prefers his mother's life and is said to enjoy playing bridge with her at her house in Cheyne Walk.

Currently Jasper has a Spanish girlfriend with a little boy he is thinking of adopting, but he shows no stirrings towards marriage.

It is Jasper's sinister gift that while his hangers-on fall apart he goes on looking radiant. Perhaps all he needs is a George Eliot heroine to reform him, but I warn you, he's persuasive. Aspirers to his hand must have a strong liver, an Irish wit and the stamina to live up to the Guinness motto, 'Happy, Lucky, Silly and Rich.'

this kitsch,' she said dryly. She becomes cool at any suggestion of pressure. Backing her up are a flotilla of inscribed photographs on the grand piano of Prince Rainier and Princess Grace, Philippe Junot and the Pope. Her eyes glowed as she heaped great rows of pagan pearls round her neck for the picture. 'I love costume jewellery,' she said. 'It's so much more amusing than the real thing.'

The real thing has not been that kind to Caroline. There are reminders everywhere. On the coffee table is a solid silver postcard. The engraving reads 'Philippe et Caroline. Happy New Life. Roberto Rossellini'. Now the French papers claim the 31-year-old son of the film star Ingrid Bergman and film director Roberto Rossellini is the new man in her life, but it seems unlikely. He appeared, Romeo-style under the peach arches, halfway through the photographic session, looking like a walking menswear promotion. Later he whirled her off to lunch in his bottle-green Rolls Royce.

'Robertino et Caroline?' shrieks the headline in *Jours de France*. In fact Rossellini seemed pretty low-key himself. He is, however, good casting for the kind of escort an intelligent girl would make sure she took night-clubbing after a bruising divorce.

How bruising it must have been is much more understandable when one sees Caroline at home in the dreamy pace of Monaco. All her life her status in the tiny principality gave her simultaneously unique protection and unique vulnerability. Her education compounded her naïvety rather than prepared her for the outside world. She went first to a local Catholic school in Monaco then to England to St Mary's, Ascot. It is hardly surprising that when she was unleashed as a student in Paris she was dazzled by the best of French paste — it was so much more amusing. Until that moment her father had always been in control, manipulating public relations, ready at the slightest provocation to bounce a bum across the border.

'St Mary's was a very good school but it didn't prepare me for anything,' said Caroline. 'Most of the girls went off to art courses in Italy which seemed a pretty bad omen.' Caroline was somewhat dilatory about her studies in Philosophy and Child Psychology at Paris university. She seems determined to make up for that now. There is a half-finished manuscript in the typewriter in her bedroom. She has written several short stories and an article for the *International Herald Tribune* about her childhood in Monaco. Friends say she rarely goes out except to grace a local event or wear her taffeta cape to the opera.

'People say I take after my grandmother, Charlotte,' she said. 'I must say, I'd like to be like her. She founded a nursing hospital here and worked in Paris prisons. She managed to do pretty much what she liked in an age when most women didn't.'

Certainly, the formal side of Princess Caroline's life seems to be minimal. The weekend we were there was, as it turned out, a gala weekend. The yearly Bal de la Rose at the Sporting Club was in aid of the American Hospital in Paris and had a theme — the Yellow Rose of Texas. This meant Princess Caroline had a lemon chiffon gown and matching cloak sent down from Dior and 300 Texans invaded Monte Carlo. The foyer of the Hotel de Paris on Saturday night was seething with Sue Ellen lookalikes sporting Bulgari rocks and huge hair. A programme of events was laid on by the Société des Bains de Mer to entertain them.

There was an agonisingly genteel fashion show at the Hermitage modelled by air-hostess blondes with Princess Grace buns. Everyone rose in silence as the tiny royal contingent made its way to the long tea-table. Princess Caroline picked decorously for two hours at the same cream gâteau. There was Didier Imbert's exhibition of Impressionists at the Hotel de Paris. Caroline made a late appearance here among the ten-gallon hats en route for the opera. And there was the ball itself for which 900 guests had paid £120 a ticket. All the press surging in the lobby of the Sporting Club seemed to know the form. 'You get one hit at the Royals as they arrive,' a photographer from the *Houston Chronicle* told me. 'After that you may as well split, coz the Rainier table is outa bounds.' As he spoke the threshing crowd of paparazzi parted with a roar. The royal party arrived, with just the right degree of lateness, at an unexpected entrance. Among the party was the chairwoman of the ball, oil millionaire Oscar Wyatt's wife Lynn, an extravagant blonde in a yellow Valentino dress adorned with one vast ruffled fin.

Beside her was Princess Grace in ice-blue Dior silk and creamy maquillage and Princess Caroline looking suitably regal in her yellow dress shimmering with crystal butterflies. They froze for the press in a three-minute gracious smile. Only the Prince's jowls twitched with impatience before sweeping past into the ballroom, decorated for the night with navy-blue star-light walls and 25,000 yellow roses. The *Houston Chronicle* photographer obediently went on to snap all his countrymen. 'For your information that is Henry Clay Koontz,' he told me elatedly as a raucous Texan wrinklie whirled by with Her Serene Highness. 'What does he do?' I said. 'Do? Honey, that's not the point! He's just rich. Plain, fat rich. And it was *Mrs Koontz* who taught Princess Grace how to do the Cotton-eyed Joe on their ranch in Texas!' He went on to snap furiously the whooping figure of Dallas bigwig Jan Feldman in a flashing chapeau (just divorcing her husband who has been acting for Philippe Junot in his divorce from Princess Caroline), the vice-president of Neiman-Marcus, Chuck Kehoe, and Louise (Mrs Denton) Cooley. There was a brief outburst of excitement when Giscard d'Estaing cotton-eyed by, but it was only his Houston lookalike — Marlene Finger's husband Alan. He was not the only lookalike present: Mrs Oscar Wyatt also had a doppel-gänger in Rome's Countess Donatella Zegna.

The Rainier table was more international. Their guests were Arnaud de Borchgrave and his wife, Marc Bohan of Dior, the Wyatts and the American Ambassador to Paris and they were, like everyone else, subjected first to René Bec et Son Grand Orchestre and then to a cabaret of drum-majorettes in jet leotards, bobby sox and luminous batons. Governor John Connally presented Prince Rainier with a Texan flag that had flown over the state capitol. Caviar was served. The drum-majorettes sang 'Deep in the Heart of Texas'. I found myself at the same table as a husky-voiced brunette with huge lips and a Twenties bob who turned out to be Edwina LaFarge, a Paris correspondent of *Women's Wear Daily*. At the same table too was a preposterously elegant duo from *Paris Match*. The photographer looked like a blond Alain Delon, the writer like the same actor playing Albert Camus. They snickered suavely when I said I was from *Tatler*. *'Tatt-lère?'* shrugged the photographer. 'Mais qu'est-ce que c'est que ça, *Tatt-lère*?'

'We came down to photograph Princess Caroline for the cover,' I said humbly. Their heads swivelled. 'Caroleen?' they chorused. 'You saw 'er? Et Rossellini? Was 'e 'anging arernd? Any other guys? 'Anging arernd?'

It was with instinctive timing perhaps that Prince Rainier chose this moment to have the *Women's Wear Daily* photographer, Tim Jenkins, bounced for getting too close to the royal table. He was whisked away for interrogation by a Monegasque Oddjob.

'It's too bad,' blubbed Edwina LaFarge, who as a consequence had been left with an empty champagne glass for nearly half an hour. 'How can he be such a fool as to get himself *arrested*? Are you coming on to Jimmy's?'

'I can spare one black-and-white picture of the royal arrival. When is your deadline?' asked a press officer kindly. '*Now*, of course!' wailed Miss LaFarge. 'Isn't the deadline *always* when the party's over?'

By this she meant, of course, not that the hubbub of festive Texans had in any way diminished but that the royal party had left — again, with maximum effect, just a little too early.

After the Junot affair one feels that their Serene Highnesses are giving their daughter a crash course in the art of royal exposure. Lesson one is a walled garden and Roberto Rossellini discreetly whiling away the night at home playing backgammon. Lesson two was not going on to Jimmy's. Princes Caroline leaves *that* sort of thing to Bianca Jagger these days — at any rate, when she's in Monaco.

THE HIGH-RENT HENRIES

the real men in real estate

It's no coincidence that the smart boys in London residential are exceptionally easy on the eye. The windows of estate agents in Chelsea are a pin-striped Reeperbahn of public-school talent. There's John 'Chunky' Lorimer at Winkworth's, Martin 'Chopper' Elwes at Maskell's, Michael 'Iron Balls' Duncan at W.A. Ellis, heart-throb Tim Simond at Mistral, the 'fab crowd' at Friend & Falcke, Ian 'Stewbags' Stewart over at the Berkeley Square branch of Savills, while at the Cale Street branch of John D. Wood, under the supervision of ex-Guards officer 'Gorgeous' George Pope, you can smell the Royal Yacht hair lotion at a hundred yards.

In the face of such charm how can an applicant resist? As one of the Winkworth team put it, 'If you're buying a house for 150 grand you don't want to be shown round by Joe Bloggs of Oik and Oik.' Their upmarket persona is useful for demoralising the downmarket applicant. Winkworth's, for instance, specialise in flats in the SW area between £50,000 and £100,000. 'The little couple from oop North looking for a £35,000 flat in Pimlico just isn't our scene,' one of their negotiators said, 'especially when you're on half commission with three other agents. We suggest *very courteously* they'd get a better service elsewhere.'

Opposite. Bubbly-babble: *'Of course, one's social life and family connections help sell houses,' says Martin Elwes*

Much of the clientele who saunter through Winkworth's doors seem to be laid-back landed gentry in their thirties looking for £80,000 pied-à-terres, or divorcing urban Camillas in search of smart maisonettes.

'The divorce rate has become a bite of a joke in our profession,' said a negotiator from nearby Maskell's. 'You know, one house to sell, two to buy.' It is, of course, an occupational hazard to be pounced by the vendor, or find her in flagrante delicto with a rival agent. Charles Delevingne, the hunky *homme du monde* at John German Ralph Pay, believes he has become an expert at spotting the commercial prospects of imminent divorce. 'It's a funny thing about women,' he said, gazing contentedly at the brochure of a £300,000 Belgravia mews house. 'Whenever they're going off their husbands they start doing up the house. If I meet a woman on her way to see her interior decorator I think, ahah, all is not well here. I'll soon be receiving instructions.'

Upmarket estate agency has not always been as jostling with well-connected beefcake as it is now. Before the war, hustling Henrys gravitated automatically to the City but the ensuing property booms lured them in large numbers as they recognised that a few years negotiating house sales would be good groundwork for becoming dealers.

It is, after all, one of the few professions left that requires no training, is not unionised and whose early stages pay so lamentably it often necessitates a private income to supplement a basic £3,000-a-year salary and a secondhand Renault 5. And its roots will always be firmly social. As Charles Delevingne put it, 'When you go to a dinner party there are only two topics of conversation: love life and property. Someone at the table is sure to be on the point of selling or buying a house.'

More recently the arrival of the Arabs provided a new influx of talent. Simon Agace, who started Winkworth seven years ago as an off-shoot of his brother's company, Mann and Co, went off to the Middle East with a Saudi *Debrett* and found that 'many of the

Opposite: Patio-patter: *'By the way, are you going to that party tonight at Tokyo Joe's?' asks Charles Delevingne*

chickens came home to roost,' while Andrew Langton at Aylesford's also jumped in and landed on his feet. (Aylesford's rivals say their image was helped by the fact that Andrew's father, David Langton, played Lord Bellamy in *Upstairs Downstairs* and clients were often confused into giving him a deferential nod if he happened to be loitering in the shop.) That boom is over, and the competition is all for the top end of the domestic market. 'In our business,' one of the Maskell's team said, 'it's not a question of what our clients can afford, so much as what's available. We never have the hassle of mortgages or bridging loans, thank God, but we do have to keep finding the right scale of property in what is really a very small patch of London. We had a Nigerian client the other day who already had three houses in Chelsea but he wanted one in Belgravia with a 90-foot reception room. Panic stations! I'm not sure that kind of space *exists*.'

One gains some idea of the diplomacy at work by wandering into Maskell's mushroom-coloured parlour in Walton Street where a young male negotiator is having a hard time on the phone.

'What sort of property are you looking for, Mrs Armanazi?' he is saying. 'We deal with a fairly wide, what's the word, spectrum. Quite, quite. You've seen Chester Square, I gather. That does have staff quarters and a very large south facing . . . yes indeed, but boiler rooms can be moved, can't they? Well, look, I'm going to suggest something completely different. Have you thought of going as far out as, well, *Bryanston Square*?'

At the next desk is the more mature Lady Kimberley, one of Maskell's most prized and experienced negotiators, also giving great phone. Bawling out the recalcitrant porter of a block of flats, she sounds like a female George Sanders. 'It's all that beastly chauffeur's fault,' she sighs as she slams down the receiver. 'He *does* put their backs up.' The atmosphere is impenetrably upmarket.

Big firms like Savills (which has a heavyweight country property reputation), Chestertons and Knight Frank & Rutley like their negotiators to go to Cirencester or night classes at a Central London polytechnic and preferably to be FRICS (Fellows of the Royal Institution of Chartered Surveyors) if they are ambitious to become partners. But even the big boys prefer a handsome contacts book to a clutch of diplomas.

In Knight Frank's Hanover Square headquarters the social magnet is Christopher Chetwode, brother of the present baron. His mother is a Berry and twenty of his cousins are millionaires. The Sloane Street branch has Lady Rose Nevill, daughter of Lord Abergavenny, and Richard Ford, the son of the Queen's ex-assistant private secretary; while at the Ascot office country residential keeps its end up with the Earl of Shrewsbury's 25-year-old brother, Paul Chetwynd-Talbot. Knight Frank's high-powered punters get treated to lunch with the senior partner, Sam Goodenough, in the executive dining-room. Here, a gentleman's club flavour is maintained. In the last three years there has been only one female guest — Mr Goodenough's mother-in-law.

Winkworth's, too, has its social stars. It seems to have hit on the right mixture of gentlemen players and is now the most fashionable of the smaller agents. The main attractions at the Chelsea office are Old Etonian Tom Hartley — a Clint Eastwood blond — and Toby Cholmeley, who reminds foreign clients of Lord Lucan and English clients of John Cleese.

Winkworth's newest social draw is John Lorimer, another Old Etonian and a dedicated party boy whose father was head of BP in Turkey. He joined Winkworth's after a disillusioning spell selling commodities which ended with 'a rather seedy little session with a company based in Holland'. Now he claims to bring to negotiating 'a certain boyish enthusiasm. When I show a flat I really want to please. I try and get across to the applicant that the scrottiest property can be transformed by the right designer.'

At Maskell's, because he is a bachelor, most of the onus of socialising falls on Martin 'Chopper' Elwes, ex-Ampleforth, ex-Lloyd's, ex-John D. Wood. At 32 he is a honed Heathcliff figure much in demand. When I saw him he had just returned from hunting in Galway, and was just off to Switzerland in his brother's Tiger Moth. He has a gun in a syndicate in Wales, a toboggan in St Moritz and a flat in Lancaster Gate.

'Yes, of course, one's social life and family connections help sell houses,' he said, 'but it always happens naturally. It's a very bad idea to be high-profile about it. A nice house sells itself.'

I watched some low-key salesmanship in action when I accompanied Charles Delevingne on a house appointment. Charles's father, Dudley Delevingne, was a famous social figure in the estate-agent world until his death in 1974. He was the toast of the Winston Churchill set in the Twenties and Thirties and gained even greater fashionability when his sister Doris married Lord Castlerosse. His son, Charles, 31, is a chip off the old blockhead, a preposterously good-looking charmer in the Roger Moore genre, who appears to move on castors.

The house he was trying to sell was a one-and-a-half-million-pounds property in a Belgravia crescent, but certainly no one could accuse him of being high profile about it. He arrived simultaneously with the applicant, a porky art dealer of Egyptian extraction who disembarked from a Rolls wearing a cashmere coat with a mink collar. Delevingne, his hand inside his jacket, royal-style, paced the part of an estate agent like an actor at rehearsal, meandering into marble bathrooms and space-age kitchens, pausing only to throw open cupboards the size of the Hilton lobby before coasting on without comment into the sauna, the discotheque and the gym. 'This is fabberless. Reely fabberless,' said the applicant.

'All the floors are Basil Spence,' said Delevingne. 'If you're feeling out of breath you might like to take the lift to the top floor.' Here he glided in and out of vast bedrooms decorated in pink satin, like wall-to-wall Janet Reger knickers. 'Somebody,' said the applicant in an awestruck voice, 'has reely got style.' It was at this moment, with a fine sense of theatre, that Delevingne produced the vendor, an Iranian businessman. He was sitting like a James Bond villain in an office hung with Picassos and Renoirs in a hitherto unrevealed suite, subtly smiling and smoking a Davidoff cigar.

'Charles, I love it,' said the applicant, when we emerged into the street. 'For the price it's good value. But it's just beyond my range.'

'No it's not,' chuckled Charles as the Rolls disappeared from view, 'he's just flogged his own flat for a million. Give him a month and he'll be back. Fortunately, none of us is in a hurry. By the way, are you going to that party tonight at Tokyo Joe's?'

In a world so dependent on contacts and charm there is nothing to prevent the polished maverick opening for business on his own. Chelsea now has a rash of smaller agents all trading recklessly on the old school tie. They can be found every lunchtime genially rubbishing the opposition in Draycott's Wine Bar or Beccofino's restaurant in Draycott Avenue or Bewick's in Walton Street. After six o'clock they haunt the Shuckburgh Arms in Denyer Street or the Admiral Codrington in Mossop Street. Here the cross-talk is so rich in names of rivals it sounds like Cockney rhyming slang. 'Been into McKenzie Ide lately? Looked to me like a touch of the Grievson Eves.'

'Johnston & Pycraft more likely.'

'Friend or Falcke?'

'Jackson-Stops actually, and this one's on me.'

The break-away boys are not welcomed by the old guard. 'The bucket shops are something we have to live with,' said Major Timothy Tufnell, one of Knight Frank's most prized country operators, 'But reputation is as important as contacts. We land the big contracts with the banks, the great estates and the commercial institutions. That takes years of integrity and competence. It doesn't come by just poncing around.'

Tim Simond, the brains behind Mistral in Burnsall Street, ran into severe suspicion when he went solo three years ago. He'd already worked on the international commercial side at Knight Frank's Hanover Square branch, valuing chocolate factories in Belgium, then a spell at Aylesford's under the hassling charisma of Andrew Langton. At 28 he is an airy, well-proportioned charmer within easy access of anything blonde. He talks with the emphatic self-confidence of the Old Etonian who has vaulted over his class. In fact, his whole air of immoderate well-adjustment is enough to plant a chip on the shoulders of Prince Charles.

'Everyone pyoo-pyood the idea I could make a go of things alone,' he told me over lunch at San Frediano's, 'which was *virry virry* silly of them. I started Mistral with a card table and a telephone and it was a long time before anyone took me seriously. One would ring up the other agents and say, "Mistral here," and have to put up with a lot of remarks like "Mistral? You mean a lot of hot air?" One battled on.'

Surprisingly, considering his background, establishing credibility with the other agents was a persistent problem. There is an unofficial cartel that shares instructions on houses and splits commissions. If

ATTRACTIVE PROPERTY
FOR
SALE
MISTRAL
351~3131

an agent fails to sell a house in two weeks, copies of the instructions are sent out to 50 or so handpicked fellow agents in the area. Getting on the list is as difficult as getting into White's. Moreover, once in the club the new member's professional manners are monitored by the others. Two agents, one of them 'a fly-by-night Iranian', have had the word put out already on them this year and been struck off the list for touting for business.

'John D. Wood refused to share instructions with us at first,' Simond said. 'George Pope there didn't like my hair. My car, as well, caused one *hell* of a kerfuffle. At the time it was a Ferrari Boxer. Now it's a Le Mans Porsche rebuilt for road-going use.' Acceptance in the club developed when Simond used his hectic social life to win himself some extremely flash instructions. He has recently sold houses to David Niven and Fiona Richmond.

'I started Mistral because I wanted a more exciting angle,' he said. 'We have a little computer here. We have ridiculous T-shirts which say Attractive Property For Sale. We advertised ourselves in the *Sunday Times* by putting a huge ear in the property pages with the words, "You haven't heard of us." We didn't get a single response, but *God*, people remembered that ad!'

Enemies of Mistral say Tim Simond is 'pushy', which one comes to realise is estate agent for 'successful'. There is a prickly resentment amongst the cartel for anyone who seems too strenuously on the make. 'If you get the reputation for being aggressive it does you no good,' said Winkworth's John Lorimer. 'You have to be correct. You have to be charming. You have to talk proper. Like us. Like Maskell's. Like Friend & Falcke. Like W.A. Ellis — Graeme Scott-Dalgleish there is a super chap, one of the best. Aylesford's we all agree is getting a *mite* too hustly these days.' Lorimer is right. As a male breed the London residentials are the straight guys. Unlike the commodity broker who tends to be born with a silver spoon up his nose, the estate agent conforms.

Certainly, no one could be more conformist than the boys at John D. Wood. They take a dim view of agents who, in their opinion,

---

Opposite. Personality-pitch: *'I started Mistral because I wanted a more exciting angle', says Tim Simond*

Double-fronted: *'One knows what time of day it is. One believes in a close shave,'* say *George Pope and Andy Buchanan*

survive solely on dinner-party deals. George Pope, who runs the Chelsea office, left the army just as he was due to become adjutant of a battalion. Unlike the relaxed, fashionable air that prevails in Winkworth's and Maskell's, his office is a well-regimented hum. Pope, with his slicked-back hair and martinet style, has become something of a legend in the estate agent community.

'I think the army made a difference to one's approach,' he told me, as all around him phones were snatched up by officer-class youth in polished shoes. 'One knows what time of the day it is. One believes in a clean shave. We offer integrity here, and we do things in a *highly* competent way. We make what can be a very emotional experience — i.e., moving — very much smoother. When young chaps come in here to be interviewed as negotiators and say they like dealing with people, I groan I'm afraid. Personally I hate dealing with people, but I'm very good at selling houses. Who else is good? Oh, W.A. Ellis pass muster. You can tell the cut of their gib.'

John D. Wood are one of the thirteen agents who have put down a deposit to share a computer. They will be able to tell at a glance which property is available, where and with whom, instead of thumbing through files of crumpled instructions while the applicant gets cold feet on the other end of the phone. John German Ralph Pay have decided against the computer because they believe it will 'de-personalise' service, but amongst the younger breed there is elation at the prospect.

Will the new technology help to break the public-school cartel? 'Not at all,' said Winkworth's Tom Hartley. 'We see it as a priority to club together and keep out the cowboys who prey on the vendor's weakness. The computer will tighten things up enormously. Certain agents simply won't be asked to join.'

Major Timothy Tufnell at Knight Frank's is more sceptical of the computer's powers to clean up the act. 'Agents are always banging on about other agents being unscrupulous,' he said, 'but the truth is that no one is as unscrupulous as the man who wants to flog his house.'

'PRETTY AMAZING'

Lady Di gets her man

All the others beached Wales. Lady Diana saved him. With the coolness of a Lorelei and the freshness of a daisy this enchanting nineteen-year-old country girl out-manoeuvred every one of the worldly blondes who had failed before. Having done it she threw off those demure cotton prints and revealed a delicious cleavage. 'There's no doubt what the message was,' a fellow guest remarked of that famous black dress she wore to the opera. 'It was "Don't think I'm just suitable. I'm gorgeous as well."' It was the greatest moment of sexual theatre since Cinderella leapt out of her clapped-out scullery clogs into her glass slippers.

But now she's passed all the tests Lady Diana Spencer's need for diplomacy and self-possession has only just begun. She has needed these qualities before. Her parents' divorce was excellent training. It taught her toughness, tact and discretion all of which she'll be drawing on now. But more valuable still in confronting the problems ahead is the unexpected bonus of extreme youth. Lady Diana Spencer comes from a born-again generation of old-fashioned girls who choose to play it safe rather than have safety chosen for them. The career girls, the rebels, the bolters, the experimenters are now among the older generation. They are, in fact, the age-group of her sisters' friends, whom Lady Diana was able to observe at length and, in doing so, draw her own conclusions about the merits or otherwise of more adventurous values. As she cuts the tape, kisses the baby or waves from the royal balcony she has one unique royal advantage. She knows what she's missed and doesn't care.

SIR HARRY THE HORSE

memoirs of the Foxhunter man

Roddy Llewellyn's relationship with Princess Margaret in the Eighties is not as celebrated as, in the Fifties, his father's relationship with his horse. They may not have gone to Mustique but Sir Harry Llewellyn and Foxhunter travelled just about everywhere else together, competing in events. At night, instead of singing round the piano at Glen they had long, serious chats together in the stables. 'I felt flattered by his interest in me,' Sir Harry confesses in his autobiography, *Passports to Life*. 'He had such charming, kind eyes.' During the course of their glorious association Foxhunter never had to cancel an official engagement because of a stomach upset and he was always gracious to the press.

Today Foxhunter's hide, along with his scrapbook, is buried under a brass plaque in the Welsh hills and Sir Harry Llewellyn is very much alive at Llanvair Grange in Monmouthshire. Here he spends his time chairing the Sports Council, breeding ponies, shooting moles and rebuffing reporters from the *News of the World* who descend from time to time to doorstep him about the career of one of his two sons. Currently it is Dai's kiss-and-tell life story in a Sunday newspaper that is causing the greater aggravation. 'I think David was surprised that he took such a pasting from his friends,' Sir Harry told me as we bolted along the country lanes that lead to the Grange. 'But if you write a load of tripe in a rag like that and describe your brother as a pansy surely you must expect to run into flack. His attitude was: today's William Hickey is tomorrow's fish and chips, but I warned him all along he was wrong. I said, David, you've cooked yourself here. You should get out of England, but of course he took no notice.'

At 69, Sir Harry is a twinkly, barrel-chested old boy with Dai's quick, musical voice differentiated only by a vestigial Welsh whinny on the vowels. He drives his Peugeot as if he's on the last lap of the Puissance and gives an excited toot of the horn as we hurtle into the courtyard of the Grange.

Inside, it has the dark, old-fashioned richness of childhood home, full of casual treasures and mysterious crannies in which to play sardines. There are wooden staircases, cavernous bathrooms reached via ankle-breaking steps, Sheraton chairs and precarious piles of books and papers. The antlers in the hall are from a record-breaking Tsessebe (a bloody great bull with rumpled horns) bagged by Sir Harry on safari from Bulawayo in 1932. His study is stuffed with a lifetime's mementoes, including a shelf-ful of cowboy hats collected in his spell on a ranch at Calgary. The walls are papered with tiny black and white gallopers reminiscent of all the horses in his life — Silver Grail, 'that Beau Brummel of a beast', 'tough-minded' Ego, 'motherly' Fairy, 'rompworthy' Black Pearl, 'enthusiastic tomboy' Golden Bell and of course, the impeccably mannered Foxhunter who had 'the charisma of a great aristocrat or film star'.

In the sitting-room, Sir Harry's wife, Lady Teeny Llewellyn, a fey blonde from the famous naval family of Saumarez is on the phone to her sister in Sark. 'Isn't it wonderful,' she is saying, 'that grandpa is on a stamp at last.'

'A journalist, darling,' Sir Harry tells her. 'Come to interview me about my book.'

'What book?' asks Lady Llewellyn. 'This is what you might call Teeny's act,' explains Sir Harry. 'I hope there are lots of pictures,' says Lady Llewellyn, turning to address the Jack Russell, Tiger, in Belgravia cockney. 'Who's a silloi toiger then?' she croons.

'I'm afraid,' Sir Harry says, 'Teeny rather believes publicity is not the thing. She doesn't mind me writing a book but she thinks it's very bad if one starts to blow one's own trumpet.'

Passports to Life is certainly not a conceited book. It is simply a boisterous chronicle of philistine self-possession. 'I chose that title,' he tells me, 'because really horses have been responsible for everything in my life. It was Ego that got me into the cavalry. It was steeple-chasing that got me abroad. It was Foxhunter who got me asked to serve on all these boards.'

It was also the facility of his class. Most of the japes and scrapes in Sir Harry's book are made all right in the end by the sudden discovery of a friend at the embassy. Politics are indicated by where you play bridge. 'My father was a Liberal — he played much of his bridge at the Reform and National Liberal Club.' Girlfriends are mixed-doubles partners painted with gallant insignificance. The chapter which describes his first meeting with his wife is headed with the name of the season's horse.

Sir Harry Llewellyn was born into a family of eight children in 1911. His grandfather, Rees Llewellyn, was High Sheriff of Breconshire in 1912 and chairman of the Bwllfa steam coal company, the largest colliery of the day. His father, a master of foxhounds, was created a baronet in 1922. As a child, Sir Harry was a 'thin, mingy little person who so far had shown little interest in anything except Uncle Oojah in the *Daily Sketch*, caterpillars, butterflies, birds and birds' nests.' Despite the pessimism of a 'brains snob' called Mr Bunbury (all the protagonists have names like this: Later we are introduced to Brigadier 'Slap' White, 'Blimp' Ferris and Col Vivian 'Pudding' Williams) he passed into Oundle. Here he had a very dull time with the sons of industry, pining for the horsey people at home. Cambridge, with its wonderful range of water-pistol activities, came next, ('It seems,' laments Sir Harry, 'that nowadays it is necessary to be academically highly qualified in order to get to Cambridge'). He hunted seventeen days out of eighteen and averaged four hunt balls a week. The vac found him cutting a dash as a deb's delight. He became famed for his wizard reverse turns in the Viennese waltz.

Fortunately, there was a tutor who liked racing enough to help him scrape a pass degree. He did a spell in the family colliery business, took a team of steeplechase horses to Hungary and had a whacko war with the First Cavalry Division of the Warwickshire Yeomanry, later campaigning in the Middle East, Sicily and the Western Desert. He returned to the colliery with the serious intention of becoming an international showjumper. For this he needed the best horse in England and found him in Foxhunter, a rich, golden bay gelding whom he bought for £1,500. Together they rode to glory in event after event culminating in their bronze medal for Britain in the Helsinki Olympics in 1952. Foxhunter became a national heart-throb. The *Daily Express* ran a hoofprint service for all the fan letters demanding his autograph. He died in 1959 aged nineteen, in a tear-jerking scene on page 220.

Llewellyn was bought out of the colliery business by the 'daylight robbery' of the Cripps Levy in 1945 and since then has concentrated on his three farms, selling ponies and his activities as a committee man. He was one of the founding members of Television Wales and

Rosie Boot's Guide to London Bachelors

Simon Oakes

Don't tell me you haven't met him yet. Ever since his first appearance on the social scene in '79, trying to crash the Charles Stevens set, there have been more and more sightings of Simon Oakes. Whether it's at the Aspinall ball wearing his winged collar and leopardskin walkers or lathering a blonde's ear at Feelings, he does seem to be everywhere.

He's not a banker, which is something. In fact, everyone agrees that Oakes's Bohemian job as front-of-house man for *The Comic Strip* is rather amusing. He has been there since it opened and will catch some of its reflected glory when it moves into the West End this October. Now he hopes to strike lucky twice and open a cabaret theatre — 'not naff Noël Coward songs' — in Soho using some of the *Comic Strip* talent to entertain the diners. Such theatrical savvy is rather surprising, considering Oakes's youthful confusion. The 24-year-old son of a Lancashire 'industralist', he went to the Jesuit boarding-school, Stonyhurst, then headed for Bristol where he teamed up with Bath bum Cosmo Fry — and got a best-forgotten degree in law. He tried journalism first but was turned down as a sub-editor by *Harpers & Queen* — 'My theory was I was over-qualified' — and only stumbled on *The Comic Strip* through a chance meeting at the Edinburgh Festival with producer Peter Richardson (it is a curious fact that the comics at the *Strip* are the only people in London who don't find Oakes funny).

Developing apace with his theatrical career have been his vaunting social ambitions, which culminated in his appearance as a blue fairy 'with lots of good accessories, you know, like weird shoes' at the Fabers' theme party in Lambeth. He is certainly a very personable escort in the wet-smack genre with a sympathetic and insistent chat-up line — 'You're so sensitive, I understand you', etc. — and a particularly effective glaucous gaze. I am here to tell you, however, that his melting approach conceals an astonishing pre-happy hour horniness that has earnt him, among other nicknames, 'Any time Oakes'.

If you want to go Dutch at the Escargot and drive him home to Fulham I suggest you audition next Friday, but it's my belief it will need a smash like *Hello Dolly* to make it worth sporting Oakes.

West. 'Lord Derby was the chairman. Lord Goodman was our solicitor. I represented the minority shareholders. We had ten glorious years.' As chairman of the Sports Council he is proud that the riders were the first to revolt against the Moscow Olympics. 'None of them wanted to go to that damn barbaric place.'

Dai and Roddy get short shrift in the book — a few cryptic paragraphs ending with the gloomy postcript: 'My two boys are well into their thirties and live their own lives.'

He seems particularly irritated by Dai's suggestion in his *News of the World* memoirs that the family are sycophantic to royalty. 'One isn't sycophantic,' he tells me. 'One just sticks to the rules, because it's so much easier. I'm not going to slap Princess Margaret on the back and say, 'Hellow Maggie. How's tricks?'' It's just affectation. I remember when Dai was younger he used to say, I saw Anne Windsor at a party last night, meaning, I suppose, Her Royal Highness Princess Anne. Well quite honestly what does it *prove*?' He blames London for Dai and Roddy's careers. ('They should have stayed in Wales with their roots.') In Roddy's case he believes he has a fatal overdose of charm. 'He's like his mother in that. You've no idea,' he adds darkly, 'the kind of people Teeny finds it in herself to be charming to.'

Perhaps the most irritating factor of all is that in the last five years Sir Harry has been better known for the social antics of his sons than for his sporting triumphs on Foxhunter. As if to remind me of this, he takes me at the end of the day to the windy hill where Foxhunter is buried. As we arrive, a Welsh daytripper is already studying the plaque appreciatively.

'I was the chap,' Sir Harry tells him at last, 'who rode that horse.' An expression of wonder appeared on the Welshman's face. 'Flaming heck!' he cries picturesquely, 'Not Col Sir Harry Llewellyn himself! Let me shake you by the hand, man.'

Sir Harry gives a soft triumphant whinny. 'You see what I mean about Foxhunter,' he says happily. 'Still pretty damn famous aren't we!'

JERRY HALL

Texan hugs and rock 'n roll

Jerry Hall's chief charm is a ten-gallon voice. She talks in a hyperbolic Texan wheedle, full of capital letters and trash-mag screamers. Friends say the only place she doesn't seem glamorous is Dallas.

'Life with Mick is just so . . . EASY!' she tells me, as she towers into the tea room of the Westbury Hotel and turns every head. 'If he says, OK, we're goin' to London ah just . . . CALL UP THE MODEL AGENCY and let them know ahm comin'. I choose to work because my ranch is so . . . EXPENSIVE! This year, ah've bred with the top rice horses and the stud fees are KILLIN' ME!'

She's 24 now and has been a top model since the age of eighteen, able to command a fee of over 1,000 dollars a day. When you meet her in the flesh it's hard to understand why. She has snaggle teeth, and size nine feet and the face of a Grand National winner but once behind the camera she becomes the ultimate prairie rose. Some of it is to do with self-projection, as well as camera angles. While Bianca was a mysterious beauty in the classic tradition, everything Jerry says and does has the ingenuous impact of a wild cartoon. Those legs swing out of an enormous car, followed minutes later by all that hair and dazzling, healthy smile — Varoom! It's Jerry Hall!

'She loves jewels and furs and travelling first-class,' an old friend told me. 'On her it doesn't seem tacky.' Perhaps this is because throughout her romances with two rock stars, Bryan Ferry and Mick Jagger, she has never been a kept woman. 'One of the reasons Mick's so gone on Jerry,' one of the Jagger entourage said, 'Is that she's the only girl he's ever had who doesn't go shopping and send him the bill.'

She had just landed the Revlon Flex Balsam contract, which meant three days' work for 50,000 dollars, and the Charlotte Ford jeans contract, which took her a day and a half for a fee of 30,000 dollars. 'Ah do believe,' croons Jerry Hall, 'that a girl should pay for her own diamonds and telephone calls and never be ashamed to ... BARGAIN!'

Her father was a truck driver who ferried explosive chemicals across America, and her mother is a medical records librarian, but Jerry was always brought up to think rich. She was the youngest of four ravishing daughters who all married too young to hit the big time, or get out of Dallas. 'Everyone laughed when I wore my sisters' falsies,' Jerry recalls. 'But later on ah was the first *Cosmo* nipple cover.' Her mother, Mrs Marjorie Hall, was determined that the same marital fate should not befall Jerry who, with her waist-length yellow hair, interminable legs and positive thinking had clearly been born to marry J.R.

At sixteen, however, Jerry had other ideas of an exit. 'Ah always thought the French were real glamorous,' she tells me. 'Ah took French lessons at high school and ah always dreamed about goin' there. Then ... one day ... in mah last year at college ah had a car accident and had a sinus membrane blocked but the compensation was 800 dollars! Ah bought a backpack and a sleeping bag and my mother made me all these ... INCREDIBLE CLOTHES that were all French copies and ah ... STUFFED THEM IN MY BAG and went to St Tropez because ah'd heard this was really the place to go and ah stuck around on the beach with this back-pack which was REAL heavy because of all the Givenchy copies my mother made STUFFED INTO IT. Then this guy came up to me and said he owned a model agency in Paris and why didn't ah join him. WELL ... he was Claude Haddad who owned the Euro-planning agency where ah stayed five years and THAT was HOW IT ALL BEGAN!'

Not quite all. Jerry swiftly became a popular model but what she wanted to be was a star. She teamed up with the Jamaican Grace Jones (later known as America's disco queen) and embarked on a campaign of nocturnal outrage guaranteed to get her noticed. 'We were so terrific together,' Grace Jones remembers, 'Her so tall with all that hair. Me so tall and with no hair. We worked all day and went partying all night. We'd dress up in bits and pieces we bought from a second-hand clothes stall called Rag Queen, covered ourselves with glitter and put it all together with tons of style.' Blonde Jerry and black Grace boogied themselves to pieces waiting for the break. It finally came in the shape of Antonio Lopez, the fashion artist who spotted Jerry one night in the Club 7 in Paris waving and drowning with a trio of impoverished actors. 'She was wearing huge platform shoes that made her about six foot eight inches tall,' Lopez told me, 'and she had a fringed paisley tablecloth round her waist, a scarf round her top and these long, dangling earrings. She was perfect, just like on my drawings. She said she was going on a model trip to India and I told her to call me when she got back. A couple of days later I ran into her. Her trip had fallen through. It was just around Christmas and she seemed very low. She asked if she could use my phone to call her family in Texas. I thought she was great and decided to push her.'

Jerry lived with Lopez for two years in St Germain. 'Mah social life was mainly gays and transvestites at that time,' she tells me, 'but nothing bad ever happened to me. Antonio looked after me real well.' He introduced her to Guy Bourdin and Helmut Newton, who found her too plump and gawky at first, but came to rate her as one of his top girls. She appeared on the covers of all the top magazines. 'Helmut did these photos of me with all these whips and chains and things. It was . . . GRYAT.' She and Lopez were briefly engaged but he knew it wouldn't last. 'I saw all along that Jerry needed to be rich,' he told me. 'Wealth is part of her glamour. I couldn't give her that but I was able to introduce her to the people who could. I knew she could take care of herself. She believed she was protected by a guardian angel. It looks as if she was right.'

Jerry met Bryan Ferry when he was searching for the girl of the moment to appear on the cover of the new Roxy Music L.P. He saw her photograph by Norman Parkinson in *Vogue* and had her flown to London immediately. She was nineteen and arrived at the airport in a ground-length sable coat. They lived together for two years in Ferry's house in Holland Park and he was devastated when, during his tour of Japan, the rumours reached him that Jerry had been seen in New York with Mick Jagger. She had met him at a model's party in Manhattan and struck him as a breath of country air after Bianca's bullchic. 'No one could accuse Jerry of being a pseudo intellectual,' a friend of Jagger's said. 'She just adores him and is always beautiful and funny and prepared to do anything. They jog together in Central Park and ride bicycles and cook. She gives him plenty of freedom but always puts him first. And she buys him presents which must be a first as far as Mick's concerned.'

'Well ah just find Mick's life REAL EASY to live with,' Jerry repeats and then goes on to describe what to me sounds a nightmare social marathon. 'It's really gryat to travel round with Mick. We stayed on Sam Spiegel's yacht this summer in France. Everyone went to bed SO EARLY it was just like being back at SCHOOL. We stayed up real late with Natasha Fraser and Christobel McEwen, you know, gigglin'. And then we take Jade and my two nieces to stay with Colin Tennant in MUSTIQUE and we always go to Trinidad carnival with NORMAN PARKINSON. We dance ... and get real drunk. In Paris we go to all these ... DRESS-UP PARTIES. Ah can really wear mah ball-gowns in Paris. When Mick's recordin' it's real easy. Ah'm leaving for work at 9.30 just when he gets in from recording. We have breakfast together and he goes to bed. Then, ah come in at 5.30 and go to sleep till 11.30 and then we go out for dinner and ah go to the studios till about three and leave him there and go back to bed. London, ah like to go to the greyhound racing at White City, and we had a real good time at ASCOT this year with Charles Benson. In New York, well that's mainly Mick's Rock'n'Roll friends, real casual. Weekends I go to MA RANCH outside DALLAS. Ah go on my own so ah can let myself go and get real dirty and not have to wash mah hair. Mah sisters come over with their boyfriends and we party and ride around on the horses and swiyam. Ah sometimes take one of 'em back to New York with me. Mick really likes 'em around. You know, TALKIN' ABOUT MAKE-UP — it makes him laugh.'

She wants now to break into films. She had a small part in John Travolta's *Urban Cowboy* and is just about to make a Muppet movie with David Bailey's wife, Marie Helvin, a close girlfriend of hers. Oddly enough, since Marie is an exotic-looking Hawaiian, the two girls closely resemble each other, perhaps because Marie also has the go-getting geisha mentality offset by a warm hank of hair and a lullaby voice. 'Imagine being married to any of those,' commented David Bailey when he last saw the two of them crooning at each other at a party.

Most people think she'll marry Jagger when his divorce from Bianca comes through. She appears genially puzzled by Bianca's financial fight. 'Ah can't UNDERSTAND why she should need Mick's money,' she says. 'Why, she could have put her NAME to a perfume or something and made herself real rich.' Bianca too, I suggest, could command high modelling fees if she was prepared to work like Jerry. 'Oh ah don't KNOW,' says Jerry silkily. 'Bianca's 34 now, you know . . .'

Others think Jerry can do even better than Mick and might even marry oil after all. She knows the importance of her roots, investing all her money in her 200 acres near Dallas. She hasn't forgotten the early struggle in Paris. Recently Mick Jagger gave a birthday party for her at Manhattan's River Café. Amongst the rock'n'roll stars and the entire cast of Andy Warhol's factory were the three impoverished actors (all established now) she'd been dancing with that night in the Club 7. That says something nice about Jerry Hall.

THE MET SET

Mrs Vreeland's big night out

Diana Vreeland's annual party to launch her latest exhibition at the Metropolitan Museum of Art was, as usual, the social peak of New York's winter season. Prancing Halstons vied with furry Fendis and capering Calvin Kleins for media attention. Marisa Berenson hoisted her shimmering silver gown and returned to the bottom of the floodlit marble steps *three*

Opposite. Diana Vreeland, Bill Blass, Marisa Berenson, Richard Golub, Joe, Estée and Evelyn Lauder. Above. Dr and Mrs Henry Kissinger, The Duke and Duchess of Bedford, Patrice Calmette and Diana Ross.

---

times to make sure the NBC camera crew had covered her entrance. America's first ladies rattled their rocks at each other under the decorous umbrella of art.

'It's a good crowd this year,' the Met's PR man told me as we awaited the first limo. 'It's not just the elderly richies and the fags. We've got the Kissingers, the Duke and Duchess of Bedford, Evangeline Bruce with Bill Paley, Diana Ross, Paloma Picasso and this year we're making sure the A group don't mingle with the Bs so it's a double whammy.' How was this accomplished? It seems the A group who all paid 350 dollars a head were to be served cocktails in the American wing, dinner in the reflecting pool room and then led into the temple of Dendur for dancing. The B group were to arrive at 10 p.m. but stay in the great hall and, he kept assuring me, unlike

Vicomtesse de Ribes, Carolina Herrera, Valentino, Barbara Allen, Bill Paley and Evangeline Bruce

last year the two crowds would *never mix*. A shuffle of the A group's dinner placement cards showed that even the Zs passed muster — Zipkin, Zarem, Zauderer, Zilker — while the Ws boasted a Wyatt, a Warhol and a Welch.

The heads of each table swept down the red carpet followed by a quadrille of guests — a suave back-swept Halston with Bianca Jagger and a glittering troupe of 'Halstonettes', the tiny sparkling figure of Estée Lauder strutting ahead of the family firm, Mrs Vreeland herself being legendary in a dramatic black Givenchy studded with gold coin dots on the arm of Bill Blass . . .

This year's exhibition is the Eighteenth Century Woman but the fashion theme of the gala guests was more Elizabethan. The vogue for jewelled Adolfo bodices, ballooning quilted sleeves (puffed up at intervals by surreptitious balls of tissue paper), short, shingled hair and gold Bulgari clutch bags created a regiment of deflowered Virgin Queens who looked as if they'd spent the last year pumping iron.

Rebels from this look cut the most dash — Evangeline Bruce in a 25-year-old Balenciaga. Nancy Kissinger playing it down in a brown print Trigere dress and fur-trimmed jacket. Diana Ross playing it up in a riot of off-the-shoulder turkey feathers. Veterans of the party chose the pre-dinner cocktail hour to slip away and view the exhibition of 125 costumes, the pièce de résistance of which is a 1759 wedding dress with a pannier skirt that measures six feet across. But most of the guests preferred to mingle with the modern-day museum pieces knocking back champagne in the American wing. There was Bill Paley frisky, sun-tanned, and smiling with all his own teeth. Eugenia Sheppard like a tiny concertina in a scarlet pleated Cardin blouson, Claudette Colbert being camera shy on the arm of Douglas Fairbanks Jr.

By nine o'clock every puffed sleeve had winged its way into the reflecting pool room for dinner leaving the statues expectant and the quartet tuning up. Outside a distant buzz heralded the arrival of the 100-dollar crowd — excited model girls, blasé journalists, rising photographers, eager fashion students, fringe pop stars, undiscovered actresses, outlandish make-up artists, all unaware that the evening's social apartheid meant their designer glad rags would only be for the benefit of each other. Useless next day when they read about their segregation to offer the solace that in the eighteenth century New York hadn't even been invented. After such knowledge, what forgiveness?

Meanwhile, as they swim up the red carpet into the great hall ready to dazzzle, the eyes of the B group are full of hope.

'YOU BRITISH ARE GREAT AT THE PAST'

how US tv saw the Royal Wedding

OK. Let's dump the sun-burst and go with the Scotch Guards playing the *Today* signature tune.

'Tina, when I point at my watch, that means we've switched into Honolulu so you can sit around and bullshit.

'Save your best gags for New York but try to keep a few for the West Coast.

'We'll start with a clip of the wedding gifts, go over to the Muppets, then you and Robert come in with why the Queen won't abdicate.'

Appearing as royalty expert on NBC's *Today* show was a far cry from *Call My Bluff*. I draw this analogy because until my seven-hour marathon under the bunting outside Buckingham Palace in front of 35 million Americans virtually my sole TV experience had been on the losing side of the Beeb's courtly quiz show where everyone sticks to their index cards. 'Follow that fact!' I wanted to shout, as I heard Earl Mountbatten described as Prince Charles's grandfather, but it was gone, vanished into the black hole of American air-space.

It was not as if the *Today* show was short on research. On the eve of the Royal Wedding a kilo of unbound Lady Diana data exploded through my letter-box. It was followed an hour later by a phone call from the production office. 'The extra tidbits for tomorrow's show should be with you by midnight,' a voice said. 'What tidbits?' I squealed. 'Tidbits,' she repeated. 'You know, asking price for Union Jacks in the Mall, weight of wedding cake, the movies they're

Passing the Buck House: *Tina B., Jane Pauley and Tom Brokaw go down 35 million American tubes*

showing on *Britannia,* crowd temperature in Toxteth.'

I sat up all night revising feverishly. How, for instance, would I recognise the Prince of Denmark? Would he be played by Derek Jacobi or Jonathan Pryce? Who was Lady May Abel Smith when she's at home? And how could I get some dirt on the Duke of Fife? Worse, how could I somehow relate it all to the American obsession with urban relations? Mercifully, most of the pre-wedding interviews had taken a psychological turn. 'Tina, do you think Lady Diana's flight from the polo field was just a cry for princely attention?'

NBC's *Today* show had been camped for a week in the trees at Canada Gate on a podium painted D.O.E. green. My first pre-wedding broadcast with Robert Lacey had taken place under giant umbrellas in pounding rain. ('No seriously, Tina, it gave it a lot of English charm.') The resident reporting team were the steel-eyed heart-throb, Tom Brokaw, and Jane Pauley, a warm, self-possessed blonde, who only lost her poise (as did we all) when she found that no hairdresser had been laid on in the caravan. 'You know I wear my hair in a Dutch roll,' she challenged the production manager. 'Can't you just wear it loose and beautiful?' he pleaded. 'Middle America does not want me loose and beautiful at breakfast, Charlie, and *you know it.*'

Brokaw, in contrast to the human Pauley, is famed for his West Coast cool, stepping off the Concorde in a pale suit and an uncreased tan all ready to ask a difficult question. At the American Embassy's party the night before he had cruised past Nancy Reagan only to be called back and kissed. 'I'll dine out on this circus for a month,' he said, cruising off again with a harsh laugh. Later Mrs Reagan engaged him in conversation with a smile that screamed for his ratings. It soon became apparent that he was not a natural royalist. 'Let's talk about the size of Lady Diana's feet,' he said in one commercial break or 'message'. 'I mean she's got gunboats down there.'

Apart from Brokaw and Pauley there were a fleet of Rons and Stans and Charlies behind the scenes, all of whom seemed to be called a vice-president. It was only at the wedding-day rehearsal, when a plump figure in rimless glasses stalked onto the set and barked, 'Robert, you talk. Tina, you smile,' that one began to glimpse the Bottom Line.

For NBC the Royal Wedding was a ratings battle with a vengeance. Their platform certainly occupied a prime site. Behind it was Buckingham Palace and the Shakespearian mob in the Mall. To the right was BBC scaffolding. To the left was ABC. As Peter Ustinov remarked, it was rather like being on a yacht in Cannes harbour. Guests on rival channels leaned against the railings and bitched about their hosts. 'Twenty years of journalistic experience just to say "the bride looks radiant",' Nigel Dempster called bitterly from his make-up caravan, while on our own set Lady Longford got a quick comb-out and Robert Lacey spent commercial breaks writing royal copy for the *Sunday Times*. There was a brief rattling rumour that our rival Barbara Walters had got the Queen Mother on ABC, but this was soon replaced by more pleasing news. A technical fault had plunged Walters into headphones like earmuffs for twenty minutes of her show.

Anyhow, who could beat our combination? For such moments of longueur as the signing of the register we had the grass-roots colour of Michael Caine in Langan's Brasserie ('He comes from Brixton which has quite a lot of relevance to your racial problems right now'), the intellectual thrust of Huw Weldon wielding a papier-mâché model of Buckingham Palace, Tom Courtenay being serious about British theatre and, glory of glories, Kiri Te Kanawa, whose dress shields had worked overtime in a limousine dash from St Paul's. ('And we'll be right back after this message.')

One felt the Americans were determined to make up in showbiz for what they couldn't provide in form. The Beeb's superiority had

Rosie Boot's Guide to London Bachelors

Martin Amis

Yes, girls, he's back. After a year in tax exile the tiny ironist who gave you *The Rachel Papers, Dead Babies* and *Success* has returned to break hearts the length and breadth of Great Turnstile Street.

Amis, 30, is the writer son of Kingsley Amis and stepson of Elizabeth Jane Howard. He read English at Exeter College, Oxford, and his flash line on Andrew Marvell won him a formal first. It is part of Amis's self-parodic mythology to pretend he was a sexual flop at Oxford. Don't be deceived. He was already smart enough to be squiring Gully ('Sophisticated? GOD, I'm sophisticated') Wells, the backless-dressed step-daughter of A.J. Ayer and cocky enough (to use Amis slang) to 'aim', i.e. dump her just before finals. He went on to work on the *Times Literary Supplement* and the *New Statesman*, where he specialised in infuriatingly self-assured carve-ups of his elders and inferiors written in the faux-donnish tone he nicked from Nabokov.

He succeeded Claire Tomalin as literary editor of the *New Statesman* and proceeded, in between writing novels, to bowl his way through an extraordinarily high proportion of London's more literate female talent whom he usually kisses off with a book dedication.

Amis's chief charm is his voice — a rich, iconoclastic croak — and the disarming boyishness of his fringe, which often causes his conquests to forget the austere, uncharitable intellect behind. As a result, they are often startled to find their pillow-talk parodied on the lips of some fresh sexual grotesque in his latest novel.

Amis is the source of huge envy and resentment from those who don't know him, particularly since he hoofed it into tax exile with a £20,000 cheque for re-writing a duff Kirk Douglas movie. Those who do know him, however, love him for his originality, his wit and his readiness to paint himself as ridiculous.

But do remember, girls, all his relationships end badly after six months and he'll paint *you* as ridiculous.

definitely got up their noses at the media briefing the previous weekend. Like the monarchy itself, a royal wedding is a great leveller. Even Barbara Walters and David Frost couldn't afford to be exempt from Aunty's briefing. They queued dolorously for their tea and biscuits and press kits along with international telly hacks of every denomination. The producer of the BBC's wedding coverage was a martinet northerner who rocked to and fro as he outlined his months of military planning. 'We are in a unique position to offer coverage which flashes from Buckingham Palace to St Paul's, back to Buckingham Palace, and then across the Mall,' he told us triumphantly. He was followed by the urbane commentator Tom Fleming, who ran through the shooting script carriage by carriage. 'Excuse me,' asked an American, 'isn't Lady Diana's coach a major security risk? We are told it is extremely fragile.' 'It's not all glass and it isn't drawn by mice, if that's what you mean,' said Fleming. National stereotyping was rampant at this briefing. The Germans asked about timing. The Americans asked about assassination attempts. The Italians never understood anything and the English asked about cost. Everyone, however, was worried about detailed identification of what the shooting script termed 'minor royals'. 'You just say two carriages of Gloucesters and Kents,' Fleming breezed, 'and hope there is no slip of the tongue.'

As it happened, the only slips of the tongue on the wedding day were Lady Diana's, when she muddled up Prince Charles's Christian names, and HRH making a pig's ear of his worldly goods.

After all the feverish boning-up we didn't even see Lady May Abel Smith, let alone the divorced Duke of Fife. What we did see on the sun-blurred monitor was a dazzling display of non-racial relations. 'You British are certainly great at the past,' Tom Brokaw said, as behind us the hot crowd waved their Union Jacks at the glass coach and screamed for the queen. 'But what about the future?'

America can relax. Toxteth will be back, Tom, right after this message.

LIFT - OFF

the fabulous life and times of the Baron and Baroness di Portanova

There is no doubt that when Baron Enrico di Portanova met Sandra Hovas, the daughter of the furniture-chain boss from Houston, at one of the city's museum balls, he had found his ideal partner. She thought so too, after seeing him in Rome in riding dress. They married in London on 20 July 1974, the anniversary of the first moon walk. Physically, they complement each other perfectly. At 53, Ricky di Portanova is a Latin playboy in the Cesar Romero genre. He has a huge, sculpted head, lip-hugging black moustache and long, silky eyelashes that bat prosperously behind the smoke rings of his excellent cigars.

The Hollywood effect is compounded by his deep booming voice, that shows no trace either of an Italian or a Texan accent. His delivery is sonorous, even courtly, sprinkled with such remarks as 'Come come, Sandra, you jest,' or 'I must confess I am fond of the grape.'

He gently derides his Texan side for its philistine implications and encourages his wife's gradual conversion of her credit-card signature from Sandra to Alessandra di Portanova. This the gorgeous baroness is only too happy to accept. Once she was just a nice girl from Houston who showed such a flair for art after graduating from the university of Texas that she went to Rome to do Renaissance studies. Now, at 33, she is not just a baroness but a raven-haired physical extravaganza flashing with designer labels and diamonds. Her walk-in wardrobe at Claridge's is a frothing cavern of taffeta and tulle, of gold-thread Juliet caps and butterfly-winged hair-combs, of shimmering opera cloaks and shining sandals.

She travels with a suitcase filled with 150 bottles of different vitamins in case she should have an off-day, but this seems unlikely. Whenever her husband is present, Sandra's solicitous gaiety never flags. After seven years of marriage her 39-inch bosom still seems to shiver with excitement when she hears his basso profondo approach. Does she cook, I wondered. 'Only enough to get my darling husband to propose,' she told me. 'Since then, never.'

Today, the Baron and his Baroness commute in their Learjet, the *Barefoot Baroness II*, between London (Claridge's), Monaco (the Hotel de Paris), Paris (The Ritz), New York (the Hotel Pierre), Houston (their own house in River Oaks), Acapulco (a 26-bedroomed mansion still only half-built), Italy (their own farm), and a family palazzo in Naples. In Monte Carlo they also have an apartment, but this is used to put up the pilots. Their plane is furnished with silver goblets from Gucci, weighted playing cards made for the astronauts at NASA and a fridge permanently pulsating with Dom Perignon. 'Since we got the jet Ricky won't travel any other way,' Sandra told me ruefully. 'I want to try the Concorde and put the luggage on the jet but Ricky says *no way*. He always says the day he has to give up his plane is the day he stays *right where he is. Yes!*'

The emphatic interpretation of her husband's rules is part of the third Baroness di Portanova's dazzling marital success. Life revolves around certain immovables. 'Ricky won't take any calls before midday.' 'Ricky only drinks Dom Perignon.' 'I handle the ambience but Ricky always chooses the cuisine.' 'Ricky will never travel in the rush hour.' 'Ricky will never go to another man's office.' 'Ricky never stays long in winter climes.' I found the same tender dogma dominating the life of her girlfriends when I joined the Baroness and her chum, Baroness de Clara — wife of the hilariously rich Baron Max — on a shopping trip to Paris. In Nina Ricci's, Baroness de Clara looked stricken when the directrice produced a particularly fantastic taffeta ball-gown. 'Absolutely not!' she exploded. 'Maxi can't stand to look at purple!' While on a cultural expedition to the Louvre it became clear that Sandra di Portanova was really still window-shopping for her husband. 'I love that Rubens,' she murmured, 'but the peacocks would never do for Rick. Neapolitans are so superstitious.'

Legend has it that Ricky di Portanova was down-and-out in Italy when the news of the death of the richest oil-man in Houston changed his life. Indeed, one likes to think of him hunched over the house carafe in steaming Naples on the day he heard he was heir to the Cullen fortune, listening to the tearful guitar music he still plays in his Learjet.

Except it wasn't quite like that. True, Hugh Roy Cullen was the Baron's maternal grandfather but Ricky di Portanova — son of Lilly Cullen and her fancy Continental husband, Paolo di Portanova — had to spend years living on his wits and fighting through 'a whole bunch of crap' before he got his hands on the money. 'If you think J.R. doesn't exist you should take a look at my uncles,' he growls when asked now of these times, but one should also take a look at his lawyer. Roy Cohn — the mastermind behind Senator Joe McCarthy — went into the marathon legal battle with a gambler's chance for his client and emerged with a settlement of twenty million dollars. Cohn has since been rewarded with many spangled nights in Monte Carlo.

Ricky has always wandered about the world, long before the Learjet. He was brought up between Italy and California where his father — now an excitable octogenarian in Naples — was Italian

Rosie Boot's Guide to London Bachelors

Julian Summer

If you want an *homme du monde* you couldn't do better than Julian Summer. Ever since his exeats from Eton he's been a three-star-dinner man. Now he's taken to banking he's an even more desirable after-eight escort. If he's not ordering you a *mélange des fruits de mer* at Le Suquet, it'll be nowhere less than the Connaught, where he favours smoked salmon, followed by grouse and a brie that 'leers at you from across the other side of the room leaving you with breath that could kill a mule'. There's something refreshingly heterosexual about Julian Summer.

He was born a Belgravia baby 28 years ago. His father was the red-hot solicitor Eric Summer, who at one time specialised in divorcing famous people; his mother is the British film star Judy Kelly. At Eton his Chopin haircut and addiction to Surrealist painters and the writings of Aleister Crowley made him the toast of school dances. He went on to read law at Cambridge where his consumptive allure gave way to a more robust, dining-club appeal. He continued to develop bizarre literary tastes but mixed with the social heavies, Nick Rothschild and Greg Shenkman (now among the noisiest people in London), and he did a further three years with a firm of solicitors in the City. He qualified with only one ambition — never to have anything to do with the law again.

Instead, he joined a lorry-load of travel freaks trundling from Rio to British Columbia and endured for sixteen weeks with nothing between himself and starvation but an American Express card. At one stage he found himself in an Amazon village where mosquitoes broke all known records by biting through a Harvey & Hudson shirt.

On return he joined an investment bank as an International Executive, with special responsibility for Spain and South America. Today, the most international thing about him is his Spanish, which is liberally flavoured with French, Italian and Portuguese. All these *viajes* have changed him from a Dostoyevsky anti-hero to a polished Pancho Villa who cuts an urbane figure behind the wheel of his gun-metal grey Scirocco. The Russian streak remains, however, in his singular sense of humour. He's often the only laughing face in a tearful cinema or crematorium. Not surprisingly he shuns the company of other bankers as becomes evident when you ask him what he does and he replies, 'There are things called Eurobonds, which are what Belgian dentists keep in a suitcase under the bed . . .' At weekends he can be found shooting at the Rothschilds' in Hampshire, eating Chinese food in Soho or playing blackjack in a wide spectrum of casinos. His hobby is the Stock Exchange. 'I like really hairy stocks,' he told me Mexicanly. 'A hole in the ground with Ltd after it. You can quadruple your money, to the point where it makes gambling look like kiddies' play. I bought gold shares at the right time and got in on Afghanistan. I'm saving up for my heart attack.'

He may sound a bit macho but he's a marshmallow at heart. The hot tip from the Stock Exchange is to get in on J. Summer Ltd. A lucky girl indeed is she who cops the key to his elegant three-bedroomed house in Fulham — and pretty punters know the shares can only go up.

consul in L.A. Throughout his youth Ricky was always aware that the Cullen family disapproved of his mother Lilly's exotic love-match and he steered clear of Houston. Instead, he played his Italian side to the hilt — 'With my face, did I have a choice?' — and dwelt on the fading glories of his family's baronial past.

He attended Hollywood High School and learnt Spanish in Mexico. He flogged cars in California (today he owns a company that finds and renovates vintage cars), flirted with the restaurant business (last year he flirted with it again when he tried to buy New York's 21 club) and modelled as a heart-throb in the Italian comic-strip trash mags known as *fumetti*. 'When I first met Sandra I bought some *fumetti* to show her what they were. To my deep embarrassment I found that today they are not soap operas but soft porn.' Finally he drifted into the jewellery business, travelling to Ceylon, India and the Far East to find the best quality stones. Today the rocks round Sandra's neck may have been run up by the Bulgaris but they are all original Ricky designs. 'I love jewellery even more than oil or real estate,' he told me nostalgically.

But it was in oil and real estate that Ricky sunk the twenty million dollar windfall from Roy Cohn. Determined to 'beat the uncles', he left Italy for Houston and started promoting oil deals. 'I studied, read, talked, listened to men like Oscar Wyatt and Bob Herring, rough men but honest. I developed quite an instinct about oil but I drilled a lot of dry holes before I was lucky. Then it happened. It was at Powder River, Wyoming. They were drilling in mineralised sand, but then we took a risk and tried the mud — Sandra was with me when we struck oil.' He invested the proceeds in real estate in Mexico and Houston, a market so booming Ricky can rest his epic head for years before he needs to do another deal. 'Of course,' he told me, 'I am still in litigation in Houston, but if you want to live in the US you have to be.'

A glance at the back-numbers of the *Houston Chronicle* and Maxine Messenger's social column ('have tongue will tattle') confirms a colourfully litigious life — suing New York's Regency Hotel for the theft from the safebox of 2.5 million dollars' worth of Sandra's jewels, suing the Quintana petroleum company (controlled by some of the Cullen family) for full accounting of the hundreds of millions of dollars in family trust funds the company manages, being sued (successfully) for divorce by his second wife, a Yugoslavian actress and basketball player, in 1972 after suing *her* in 1968 for the return of a 130,000 dollar ring. 'Why, anyone would think Ricky *likes* wrangles,' the third Baroness di Portanova cries, 'when in fact my darling husband is quiet as a lamb.' Houston is still Ricky's least favourite stop-over. His rich rigmarole and imported fancies are not universally approved of in that work-ethic town. 'The Baron and Baroness Deported from Nova,' snort their detractors.

This summer Ricky was in a sombre mood after the blow-up of a new controversy. Nigel Dempster had alleged in his column in the *Daily Mail* that Ricky had secretly put up the money for Nether Lypiatt, the Gloucestershire house recently bought by Prince Michael of Kent. 'Other than the brownstone I offered to President Reagan in New York during the presidential campaign, I have never purchased a house for anyone but myself or my family,' he told me morosely. House problems seem to dog Ricky. His home in Houston, containing a Napoleonic mantelpiece, a Steinway piano and a collection of Fabergé boxes, was burnt down in mysterious circumstances two years ago. Next he found himself fiercely disputing rumours that their Acapulco house was being built for the Shah. 'We want to quelch (sic) that rumour once and for all,' Sandra told the *Houston Chronicle* (their house was vastly bigger than the Shah's).

The Baron and Baroness arrived in London, as always, for the social month of June, setting up their headquarters at Claridge's. They like their suite so much they once tried to buy it. Now it is reserved for them for three months of the year and the furnishings have been adapted to suit their taste. 'I adore the old-world atmosphere,' Sandra said. 'And since we've changed the curtains from grey to salmon it looks so much fresher.'

Their day would begin, as often as not, with lunch at Les Ambassadeurs with the gregarious Baron and Baroness de Clara. Afterwards, while Sandra might go for dress-fittings with Bruce Oldfield, Ricky would ponder whether or not to buy an art exhibit at Wildenstein or an interesting batch of Spanish guitars. Several afternoons were taken up having their miniatures painted in Renaissance costume.

Sometimes they would go to Rome for a party. Another day the

Baron lent Sandra the plane to take Baroness de Clara and myself to Paris to look for a dress for Monte Carlo's Red Cross Gala. We set off from Claridge's at 7 a.m. in the Rolls, leaving Ricky asleep. Sandra had provided him with a Sotheby's sale to attend. 'I always make sure my darling husband is amused when I'm away on a trip,' she said. 'And I never let my girlfriends know which day I'm going.' By midday we were in the Louvre checking out the Fragonard ('I prefer the one we have in Houston') and by one resting our feet in Maxims. In Nina Ricci, Baroness de Clara found her heart's desire in a scarlet ball-gown made of floating layer upon layer of flaming chiffon. It was reduced from £6,000 to £3,000 but, as we discovered, there was a sinister reason for its presence in this bargain basement. 'Yes,' the directrice said, 'I cannot deceive you. It has been seen on Madame Gérard.' By 7 p.m. we were back in Claridge's with six boxes of gold and silver tableware. 'Pressures of work alone kept me from joining your amusing excursion to gay Paris,' Ricky said when I telephoned to thank him. 'I'm glad to hear you curbed Sandra's worst extravagances.'

On rare nights without a party to go to, the Portanovas dined on asparagus and crême brulée at the hotel. More usually, evenings started in their suite and ended at 5 a.m. at Annabel's. One such occasion was a black-tie dinner they gave for the treasurer of the Conservative Party, the Hon Alastair McAlpine, and his new wife, the gourmet grocer Romilly Hobbs. It kicked off in their suite at 8.30 with a pianist tinkling Sinatra hits on their specially supplied Bechstein and £500 worth of Beluga caviare trolleying round to accompany the Dom Perignon. Sandra's fabled bosom was on display in a red silk Valentino gown and adorned with a necklace of diamonds, rubies and emeralds (the colours of the Italian flag). The other guests included a subdued Ava Gardner, escorted by her murmurous walker, the Hungarian textile designer Michael Szell; a burly German with a duelling scar, who turned out to be the Baron de Clara, with the chic blonde Doris; Sir Charles Forte's son, Rocco; an elderly American couple who have lived for 25 years at the Hotel Meurice in Paris; and an Italian count who claimed some connection I never understood with Lord Thorneycroft. Most of the conversation was about the comparative excellence of hotels. (Ricky himself never varies his beat. He once made the mistake of trying the

Marbella Club in Spain, but checked out within two hours when he discovered that room service ceased at mignight.) One of the guests observed that after the first move in one's life there is never a day when one doesn't wonder if one is in the right place. The elderly American woman grabbed his arm. 'Never a minute,' she told him hoarsely.

The party moved on to the wine cellar of Annabel's. Here, to the piped serenade of the theme tune of *Brideshead Revisited*, we washed down soufflé de homard with 1973 Dom Perignon, tornedos Rossini with 1962 Château Latour, and fresh raspberries with Dom Perignon Rosé 1969. Seated at the head of the long table, Ricky was at his most benign. Over coffee he made a touching and thoughtful little speech toasting the newly-wed McAlpines. 'If only he hadn't given up those singing lessons I know he could have been an opera singer,' Sandra mourned. 'Yes! My darling husband is so much sexier than Pavarotti.' ('Come come, Sandra, you jest.') When I left at 1 a.m. Ricky was shuffling rhythmically with Ava Gardner, and the de Claras saw in the dawn.

The Portanovas maintain this frenzied redistribution of wealth for twelve months of the year, except in July and August in Monte Carlo when they escalate it. Their passports have a permanent tan. In London they keep their chauffeur on all the year in case they need him. A different chauffeur and a small Rolls pilot them round the narrow streets of Monte Carlo. In Houston they own a fleet of vintage cars. In Italy they drive a Fiat. The fear of kidnapping is a regular conversation topic at Portanova parties. Sandra never goes shopping in Rome without a personal bodyguard. 'Unfortunately,' Ricky told me, 'the last time she took the bodyguard with her the police arrested him for following her. The foooool!' Their farm in Italy is sparse compared to the rebuilt Houston house with its collection of Tiepolos. 'Since we can't have any art there I have to make do with pets,' Sandra said. 'I had a kinkajou for a time and also two gibbons called Othello and Desdemona. But do you know what happened to that poor Mrs Gibbon? He strangled her! Yes! Never name a gibbon after a play with a bad finish!'

But the splendours of their Houston and Italian houses are as nothing compared to the on-going palace in Acapulco. You can water-ski on the swimming-pool ('Yes! It's a very small lake but a very large simming-pool.') It has 26 bathrooms, five kitchens, two further swimming-pools, guest villas for fourteen and staff quarters for fifteen. Michael Szell is flown in and out to design the fabrics. He was often whisked to Claridge's to make up a dinner four, arriving in a trice and laden with chic little gifts — Haitian fans for Sandra and a giant magnifying glass for Ricky. 'Aha,' the baron boomed, examining it intently. 'Now I can find my brain.' (Come come, Ricky, you jest.)

The Portanovas left Claridge's at the beginning of July. Bruce Oldfield flew after them two weeks later with the finished cocktail dresses. One sensed they were relieved to escape from London's baleful photobooth into the bright, shiny Disneyland of Monaco. So relieved that they celebrated soon after by throwing a party in Rome. 'My jewels are from Paris, my shoes are from London, my dress is from Rome,' Sandra sighed as she tried on a new Valentino. 'I feel very EEC tonight.'

If there's one thing her darling husband's taught her, it's that every take-off is a landing somewhere else.

ESTÉE LAUDER

heaven scent

Estée Lauder is a wonder. Any notion that the grande dame of cosmetics has become a mere figure-head in her own empire is dispelled when you visit her in the Louis Quinze sky-lab she occupies on the 37th floor of the General Motors Building in New York.

'Mrs Lauder is simply psychic,' says Miss Sadler, the PR lady who is herself a walking image of this season's Lauder Country Market ad, her brown hat fashionably tilted and her Big Sweep shawl flung over her tweed suit. 'She knows instinctively which is the correct texture for her age-controlling cream or her new fragrance. It is no coincidence that in 1978, the year China opened up, Mrs Lauder gave us Cinnabar.' She takes me on a tour of the offices, all painted Lauder blue and furnished with chaises longues, porcelain vases, Chinese rugs and chandeliers. From the giant windows you look down on the green baroque roof of the Sherry Netherland Hotel and straight into Warren Beatty's penthouse. The tour culminates in the executive dining-room where the table is laid with displays of Mrs Lauder's cosmetics and perfume ranges — White Linen, Cinnabar, Alliage, Private Collection.

'Too many women simply deal with their pulse points when they apply their fragrance,' Miss Sadler says. 'Mrs Lauder believes that the correct way to achieve a subtle, day-long allure is to spray your fragrance ahead of you, walk into it and twirl.' (Miss Sadler sprays, walks and twirls like a Victorian automaton.) 'Mrs Lauder's fragrances are all compatible with each other. She believes it is

important to strike a different note at different moments of the day. White Linen body lotion to give you that extra freshness in the elevator. White Linen fragrance at noon when you feel a little bolder. But Private Collection at night for that sophisticated date.'

'Or let me put it another way,' says a voice behind us as Miss Sadler and I fall into a reeking, exhausted silence. 'At breakfast who needs the smell of escargot?'

Mrs Lauder, just back from lunch, bursts into the executive dining-room, and helps herself to a cookie from a silver salver. She is a diminutive blonde bombshell in a Givenchy print dress and royally matching hat. 'When you go to the gym, you don't want to conjure up a symphony orchestra. That's why I invented Alliage, the perfect fragrance to go jogging.'

What about cosmetics? Is the emphasis on scent nowadays? Mrs Lauder peers at me. Her shrewd Viennese eyes narrow as she finds herself face to face with Boots No 7. 'I believe in sheen not shine,' she says. 'Sit here and I'll show you how to look as beautiful as a bride in three minutes flat.'

As Miss Sadler stands by in rueful admiration, Mrs Lauder's deft fingers fly over my face, putting on moisturiser first. Next (a revelation, this) cream rouge. Third, Polished Performance foundation. And last a blusher which she applied with seeming recklessness to such wild, uncharted places as between my eyebrows and on my chin. We all looked into the mirror and gasped. 'Beauty doesn't come from within,' Mrs Lauder says. 'It comes from putting the soft film compact rouge under the foundation. That way it puts a glow on your skin. Start the new season with a new face. Have another cookie.'

The Lauder empire is upheld by Estée's family. Her son, Leonard, is president of the company and his wife, Evelyn, is vice-president. Her husband Joe Lauder was her sustaining business guru until his death. 'Some people made the mistake of underestimating Joe,' a friend said, 'but Estée didn't make a move without consulting him.' What is plain is that it is the tiny dynamo herself who still approves, and often originates, every perfume, lipstick, powder and face cream. Some of her most inspired products — like the miniature pressed perfumes to carry in the handbag — stem from her common sense. Women don't want to carry huge clunking bottles in their bags. 'Do you know why I stand for quality?' she asks me. 'Because when you have an Estée Lauder jar in your house you have my soul on a label, not stocks and shares.' She peers into my face again. 'Yes dear, now you can go to Studio 54 and glow.'

Have you got that, girls? Rouge on first, then spray, walk and twirl — but don't forget to keep your eyes closed. The range is White Linen, not white stick.

FASTER, FASTER, LONDON GIRLS

These interviews are an attempt to clear the minds of newspaper feature writers who, every now and then, telephone the *Tatler* in their routine assignment to assassinate a group of girls they call 'debs'. What exactly do you mean by debs? I asked the most recent enquirer, an excitable woman's page columnist. 'I've got some names down here,' she said, 'Catherine Oxenburg, Christabel McEwen, Geraldine Harmsworth, Nicky Haslam ...' 'Nicky Haslam!' I squawked, reeling from all these strange bedfellows, 'but he's a man.'

'A deb's delight,' she explained, giving me no time to ask how a 40-year-old interior decorator who wears leather trousers could have ever blundered into this particular social typecasting. Or was Haslam's *tenue de chasse* bunfight in Hampshire last year really his coming-out party?

'Oh you know what I mean,' she persisted. 'The sort of girl like Natasha Fraser who's always at hunt balls and having dinner at the Savoy Grill.'

Even as we spoke Natasha Fraser was winging her way to St Tropez with freshly inked hair to spend two weeks as the house guest of the Hollywood mogul Sam Spiegel.

'I suppose what you're trying to tell me,' my caller concluded sullenly when I explained that no one under 45 has dinner at the Savoy Grill, 'is that the deb has finally died out.'

No. No. No. The deb has not died out. She is still here selling programmes at the Berkeley Dress Show. She still asks for something called 'a lattice-work belleek cache-pot' on her wedding present list at the General Trading Company in Sloane Street. She still says 'yah' and 'hice' and 'shnorkel' instead of 'snorkel' and throws a drinks party for 150 at Searcy's in Pavilion Road. She still belongs to the junior social committees of charity balls and is often snapped by Swaebe between shandies at a hooley. She's a boarding-school blonde from the shires with short, buffed nails and a wispy fringe who finally disappears back to the country with a baronet in tow after four years of committed mind-broadening in the stews of Annabel's, the casbah of Christie's, the rain forests of Fulham. In short, she's still as boring as ever.

But there is another sort of girl around — her day-school London cousin whose parents, if not aristocratic, are often in the media. She has short, scruffy dark hair, always wears black and likes to be snapped — but by Snowdon. Sex is not a 'big thing' to her. She is independent and self-possessed — since the age of fifteen she has managed her own life in a granny flat in the house of liberal parents. 'We rarely communicate except to row about the housework,' is one reprise, but the generation gap gets bridged when it comes to borrowing a ball gown or the attention of Mark Boxer. She's mobile, mouthy, racy and resilient and she wants a career.

As for her social life, it's hectic and eclectic. She draws her friends from different backgrounds and they often never meet each other. 'One knows people for a bit then they vanish or leave the country,' I was told. 'There's no central society just a collection of cliques whirling around on the edge.' The mixture of influences in her world can find her reeling in Scotland, roller-skating in Chelsea or dressing-up at Oxford. She's proud of being a chameleon and her experience with the make-up artist who prepares her for glossy pages leaves her with amazing expertise. Just when you've got used to her scuffed pumps and new-wave cow-lick she turns up in taffeta and her mother's tiara, exuding Annigoni cool.

Only one thing is certain. At night when she's in London you'll find her having dinner at Eleven Park Walk, the Chelsea restaurant where somehow they always get you in and the spiral staircase offers an amusing sideshow of up-market legs descending to the tables crammed below. Here might appear such legendary, pass-through characters as ex-Oxford libertine Jasper Guinness holding court to tumble-haired Geraldine Harmsworth and Natasha 'The World is her Oyster' Grenfell, while at another table a Dartmouth cadet who turns out to be Sophie Hicks, tries to sweep a slumbrous Evgenia Citkovitz into her yellow jeep for a midnight expedition to The Click. 'I suppose,' said Nicky Shulman thoughtfully, 'it's a long way from the world of Captain Fogie.'

Natasha Fraser

Natasha Fraser, seventeen, is the youngest of Lady Antonia Fraser's three astounding daughters. She decided this year to be the only brunette. Her eldest sister Rebecca is at New York University from where she was, until recently, squired by Bobby Kennedy.

Her middle sister, Flora, is a brilliant beauty who is reading classics at Oxford and has just married Robert Powell-Jones. Natasha herself has her mother's mouth, spiky punk hair, an enormous pair

Rosie Boot's Guide to London Bachelors

Gregory Shenkman

What about an exciting emigré for a change? Or at any rate an escort who looks like one. Gregory Shenkman is only half Russian but wholly available and in a city overrun with effeminate one-shave-a-day men he is genuinely hairy.

Shenkman, 30, is a punchy, closely-packed banker who goes off like a Molotov cocktail when provoked. He talks in a series of italicised explosions, '*God damn!*', '*Hell's teeth!*' etc, but when he simmers down becomes moodily Muscovite. He lives alone in what he describes as a 'converted tea-chest in Fulham with an expensive stereo and a kitchen which I firmly believe has a dead body in it. There is a huge bed upstairs. *God damn!*' He relapses into awed silence.

With all this directionless libido it is staggering that Greg has reached the dangerous age without a live-in companion. This may be because he has spent the last ten years remaking the family fortunes. His father was a flamboyantly rich entrepreneur with a house in Somerset and another in Ennismore Gardens, Kensington, before steel was nationalised. Greg was sent to Stowe then Sherborne but by the time he hit Trinity College Chambridge family finances necessitated a full grant. It was a character test — *Hell's teeth! What a test!* — especially after a summer spent with his father on a gastronomic tour of France 'which had just taught me ironically that there is life beyond baked beans'.

But Greg passed without much of an overdraft and a newly defined sense of Slavonic fatalism. He developed a mixed taste in friends who included *Not the Nine O'clock News* producer John Lloyd, Nick de Rothschild, the Hon Alex Catto, Julian Summer and a number of Rastafarian anarchists who wanted to put money into freedom fighting. This could be described as Greg's Frisbee period. In his third year he rediscovered his interest in history and socio-economic structures not a moment too soon for his tutors who were gratified to see him off with a high-flying 2:1.

Greg flirted with being a captain of industry then discovered what budding captains of industry are paid. Without further ado he bounced into investment banking, where he has been bouncing ever since. He has not lost his interest in socio-economic structures, however. He describes himself now as 'a flagging monetarist', i.e. he thinks Thatcher is a Bloody Fine Woman but rues the fact the free-market forces don't seen to work on their own.

Indeed they do not. Which is why I urge you to think hard about this elegible young dynamo instead of wasting precious time sticking pins into wax dolls of Lady Diana Spencer. Gregory Shenkman will make an ideal husband for a girl with a high noise threshold. Beneath his mangrove chest there beats a romantic heart. Life might be deafening but it would never be boring, and once he finds the right girl to play Russian roulette, Shenkman, I believe, is unlikely to defect.

of grabby dark eyes that sparkle with vivacity and daring. She thrusts her chin out when she laughs, causing one of her dangling earrings to whistle past her spinach salad.

Her schooling began with St Mary's Ascot but she left to take eight O-levels at Queen's College in London. She has just enrolled at a tutorial to do first her A-levels and then Oxbridge entrance. 'At boarding school girls got really heavy,' she explained. 'So did the nuns. When mummy went off with Harold they kept coming up to me with long faces and saying, "We're praying for your mother Natasha".' She was only allowed to leave boarding-school on condition she worked hard. 'When I first started going to parties I thought London was *really* glamorous. But I saw the light at Andy Warhol's party. I quite liked Andy Warhol — he seemed rather a sweet old man, but Nicky Haslam — *god.*' The earrings dance. 'Fortunately I've made some good friends — Christabel McEwen, Anna Gendel, Evgenia Citkovitz, and Ned Durham. Hugo Guinness has a sweet foolish charm, I suppose, but he's such a fascist. He's got views which even my father doesn't have. There are lots of phoney people around. The worst thing about London is the way everyone whips your quotes. I have my own lines, thank you very much.' One of Natasha's less popular lines was to describe Evgenia Citkovitz at the Rutland ball as 'looking like an unmade bed'.

Christabel McEwen, eighteen, Natasha Fraser's partner in crime, is the youngest daughter of the distinguished painter Rory McEwen and his wife Romana (née von Hofmannsthal) of Bardrochat in Ayrshire. She, too, is one of three beautiful sisters. The oldest, Flora, a much-photographed bombshell, is a dress-designer in Brazil: 'So there's no hope of you getting her into one of your articles.' The middle sister Samantha is an artist who spends half her time in New York. 'There are 200 McEwens in London,' Christabel said. 'We've been brought up to think we're Hitler's race of Aryans.' She is in fact the only blonde I spoke to, although diligent refusal to wash her hair had made this less obvious.

Christabel had roller-skated all the way from the King's Road to the Westbury Hotel in a white T-shirt and dungarees to meet me. She has just finished her A levels at Godolphin and Latymer and wants to do an art apprenticeship with Nigel Waymouth. She is

Christabel McEwen

brash and joky and optimistic. 'Something will turn up because I've got a strong fate line on my palm. I don't like people who are hopeless. I have artistic ambitions which I have no doubt I'll fulfil.' She uses Bardrochat as a crash pad to recuperate from London. 'The McEwens are rather isolationist when they get to Scotland. A hundred years ago they spoilt the Duke of Wellington's view and neighbourly relations have gone down from there.'

At night she goes dancing as much as she can. 'René Gordon Butcher takes me to Tramp. Pickford Sykes takes me to Annabel's. I don't have any one boyfriend — I'm too romantic.'

'Christabel takes awful people a bit too seriously,' Natasha told me. 'One has to accept that Sebastian Taylor has his amusing side and leave it at that.'

Nicky Shulman, 20, is a stunning media child enjoying her third year as the toast of Oxford. She is the younger daughter of *Evening Standard* theatre critic Milton Shulman and his sparky wife Drusilla, features editor of *Vogue*.

She is animated and intense with a frayed, artistic air, the kind of daunting crony the boyfriend brings home in a French film to make the heroine feel out of her depth.

'Oxford,' she says ruefully, 'is very much *à la recherche*. People are still obsessed by its past glories and invent societies like the Piers Gaveston [which celebrates dressing-up, not hot pokers or buggery] and the Assassins, whose sole importance is to those who aren't invited. I think my year is the most socially motivated for a long time. The trouble is that of the sixteen men per woman, fifteen you never see and the sixteenth is gay. Oxford is the San Francisco of England.

'I never meet the shire crowd at Oxford. A lot of the stars are second-generation media people like Piers Hodgson — Godfrey's son, Felicity Rubinstein — Hilary's daughter, and Huw Weldon's son — I think in-breeding has finally taken its toll and the nobs have gone to Cirencester which is packed with dukes, I'm told, driving tractors.'

Louise Steel, 24, is the red herring of this article, photographed to further confuse newspaper feature writers still sleuthing round the Savoy Grill. She is here to prove there are still such things as debs and they sometimes break mould, or try to. Louise Steel is a stockbroker's daughter with an American mother; she went to finishing school in Switzerland, a secretarial school in Cambridge and did a cookery course with Mrs Russell. 'I'm very interested in

Nicky Shulman and Louise Steel

bloodstock and cooking.' So far, so stereotyped. Then a friend who worked for Hambros snapped her in Richmond Park and 'somehow' the photograph found its way to Models One who took her on. She went off to New York where she shared a flat with another girl and together they drove across America to the West. She was self-supporting for two years working her way up from catalogue work to a cover for *Town & Country*. It was in New York that her spaniel-brown hair and serene grey eyes won the interest of Jamie Blandford, heir to the Duke of Marlborough. He has squired her ever since. 'It is absolutely not true what the *News of the World* wrote,' she said, ardently. 'I've never done any underwear shots and I never will.' Poor Louise Steel. She tried to be emancipated but she had reckoned without the chauvinist tabloid press who, once they've labelled a deb, like to keep her there for ever. All the solicitors in Gray's Inn will not suppress the field day they'll have when 'Jamie picks a naughty knickers duchess'.

Evgenia Citkovitz, 17, the most hauntingly pretty girl in London, has no such social pressures to bother her Bohemianism. She is the daughter of Lady Caroline Blackwood and the musician, the late Israel Citkovitz. Like her mother, who was always awash with cigarette ash and cake crumbs, Evgenia specialises in looking a beautiful wreck. She is a soft-focus brunette with vague, melancholy green eyes and a mouth like a bruised peach. She can't pronounce her R's, which adds to her seductively hopeless air. She plays the piano brilliantly and is about to sit, a year early, her Oxford entrance, which few doubt she will fail. 'I may do,' she said drowsily. 'I'm such a spowadic worker.'

Everyone is fascinated by Evgenia, partly because she's born into a richly textured family. A lot of her childhood was spent living in Ireland with her grandmother, Maureen Marchioness of Dufferin and Ava. 'So finickety,' sighs Evgenia. 'She made me go through this absurd dress rehearsal when the Queen Mother came to dinner.' Her mother's first husband was Lucian Freud, with whom she eloped when she was eighteen. Her own father died when she was ten and her mother married for the third time to Robert Lowell. 'We lived in this rambling pile in Kent with a study on top of the house where Robert worked. He was very gentle but he made the oddest comments at times.' His death after her father's was only one of the sad things in Evgenia's life. Her elder sister died of a heroin overdose at a party a few years ago.

Evgenia spent six years at a trendy co-educational school, 'which I

Evgenia Citkovitz

loved but got bored in the end because all anyone wanted to do was sit around getting stoned.' She's now doing history and music A levels at St Paul's, Nicky Shulman's old school. She succumbed briefly to the Sweet Foolish Charm of Hugo Guinness, and is now being escorted by Oxford svengali Napier Miles, the charismatic son of the keeper of the Privy Purse.

Venetia Spicer had just celebrated her 21st birthday party when we met. At the party most of the guests were so young one boy shattered 27-year-old Lord Burghersh by calling him 'Sir'. Venetia herself is a rangy, thoughtful beauty renowned for her elegant dancing. She is a deb who got away, as is plain by her mutinous glare when her mother, Mrs Paul Spicer, points out an oil painting of Venetia in ancient Greek get-up with the comment: 'Venetia is very classical.'

After doing the season Venetia split to Sri Lanka where she took

Venetia Spicer

an extended holiday with Prince Stass Klossowski. On return she played a Hawkwoman in the film *Flash Gordon*, and settled down to write and illustrate a children's book. Called *Chatrat*, published by Quartet, it is a delightful yarn about a rat who's broke and goes off to seek his fortunes abroad. It has nothing whatever to do with Prince Stass Klossowski.

'I've got a lot more travelling to do researching the next Chatrat book,' she told me. 'Egypt, I thought, to help educate children about the pyramids.' Chatrat, I predict, will go down a storm.

Amanda Grieve

Amanda Grieve, finally, is the heartbreaker of the group, famed for being original. She is 22 and just down from Somerville where she was an English scholar. She was born in NW1, the daughter of a senior partner in a law firm and an alluring mother 'who does frivolous things for the Royal Academy'. Her parents were divorced when she was eleven. 'One just got more presents at Christmas.' She now lives with her father at his house in Newbury. 'A calm, beautiful place where no one slams doors.' Here she is finishing her first novel. 'Not a Drabblish thing,' she says. 'A real novel with a plot like the Victorians.'

Amanda is a small-boned, feline girl with, inevitably, short, rumpled dark hair. She is notorious for being tricky, disappearing with no forwarding address, leaving the men who pursue her to sob on the doorstep. 'There's no doubt in my mind that Amanda Grieve has given me more trouble than any other girl I've known,' said Napier Miles bleakly.

'I'm Gemini, schizophrenic,' Amanda explained with a heartless smile. 'Napier says I'm like Florimell in *The Faerie Queene,* always looking over my shoulder, never committing myself.' Friends say this kind of remark is typical of La Grieve who drives men mad.

Now she's down she seems destined to be the Park Walk intellectual with a Sagan streak, interested not in politics but 'political structures', not in people but the 'way they interact'.

So that was Natasha, Christabel, Nicky, Louise, Evgenia, Venetia and Amanda. Now can we all please forget about Hunt Balls and the Savoy Grill?

54 VARIETIES

full of beans at Studio 54

The night Studio 54 re-opened, Manhattan's night-owls were divided into two classes, those who couldn't get in and those who couldn't get out. 'This is an exit!' screamed the doorman as twelve youths wearing feathered masks and matching loincloths and a girl in a split-crotch silver space-suit tried to burst through a backdoor. 'You're all gonna get your toes mashed!' A breakaway group who tried to enter via an underground carpark collided with a film crew trying to do the same thing. Meanwhile at the front, armed police and firehoses guarded the thrashing crowd. 'Studio 54 is filled to capacity,' a megaphone boomed. 'Please clear the sidewalk.' 'This is a real bummer,' said a teenage girl in a green varnished breastplate. 'I came all the way from Newark for this.' Further back, a sober middle-aged contingent held up placards which read, 'Studio 54 is a horror to its neighbours.' 'It's up to the man on the street to stamp out these freaks,' one of them told me.

But where in all this bedlam was Steve Rubell, the hectic midget who hyped the studio to fame and notoriety before his eleven-month prison sentence for defrauding the taxman? Mr Rubell, along with his best friend, fashion designer Calvin Klein, was hosting a pre-opening party at Klein's high-in-the-sky apartment which looks

Opposite. Full of beans: *Calvin Klein and Brooke Shields flanked by her mother, Terri Shields, and Steve Rubell. Below, two queens of the night*

down on the shimmering neon rainbow of the East River. It was like being inside the lightbox at *Interview*. As the doorbell kept ringing, in streamed Jack Nicholson, Christopher (Superman) Reeve, Debbie (Blondie) Harry, Mary Tyler Moore, Dick Cavett, Egon von Furstenberg, Nan Kempner, Michael Bennett (who created *A Chorus Line*), Divine, Fred Hughes and three dozen male models in checked lumberjack shirts and wet-look hair. While Klein cruised the room with his date for the night, Brooke Shields, little Rubell effervesced at the door. 'This is like a whole new deal for me,' he gibbered, embracing Andy Warhol. 'A new start. I'm not knocking prison. I read 400 books. I just mean it's nice to be out. Hi, Apples. Looking *good*. D'you know they put me on a floor with criminals so *hurrible* you had to call them by a code name like F3 or G7! But I'm here to tell you that the G7 crowd were nothing as bad as the white-collar criminals.'

At this point the door opened to reveal the king and queen of the New York party pack — Jerry Zipkin and Diana Vreeland. Right behind them was Halston, wearing black. The two men embraced. 'Steve, baby, looking *good*.' 'I know,' said Rubell giving his whipped-cur smile. 'Enjoy!' Meanwhile, wherever Calvin and Brooke strolled a cluster of celebs strolled too. Brooke, a beautiful tousled giraffe, stopped once to rub noses with Jack Nicholson. At midnight the hot spot in the room was Calvin's walk-in wardrobe, an abbatoir of cashmere, suede and leather, large enough to accommodate a dozen socialites asking each other, 'Are you going on?' 'I think this party proves it's the people not the place that matters,' said Rubell, who now wants to open a new discotheque in Paris. One wonders if he will exercise his old tyranny about who gets in and who doesn't. 'Steve feels kind of sore about certain people since he went to prison,' one of the models said. 'Some of his close friends forgot to write.'

WHAT A KOO

Stark by Parks

Will somebody *please* take Koo Stark seriously? This girl can do Big Thinks on any subject under the sun, even wild-life. 'A lot of people are so concerned about endangered species,' she told me. 'They seem to forget there are a lot of neurotic cats and dogs around.'

We were talking over lunch at Brown's Hotel at the end of a trying week for Koo. Since the royal story broke last year she has been living out of a suitcase, dodging the press. Even her cockatoo, Candida, which travels in the basket on the back of her bicycle, has been misrepresented. It appeared in the *News of the World* as Alice, a parrot she's training to say, 'No comment.' All this harassment has been something of a strain for a young actress in search of a testing role. She's not interested in being a model and for fashion work she is, in any case, too small, a pocket Venus with such a tiny waist *Tatler's* fashion team had to clinch the back of her ball-gown together with a giant bulldog clip before she sank without trace in the tulle.

No, it's the big screen now for Koo, which is why it's such a bind that producers wishing to contact her to offer her parts have had to queue outside her digs along with the paparazzi. 'Some actresses just want to do classics but I wouldn't want to be typecast,' she said. 'I read a lot and I've noticed there are a lot of very good parts for women. That new book *White Mischief* has got one for a start. *I Never Promised You a Rose Garden* was a great classic with another very good part, but the trouble is, I think that one's been done. What I'd really like to be is part of a creative think-tank, with a group of other actors, writers and technicians.' So far the best script that's got through to her is about a female hitch-hiker with enormous thumbs. 'I'm definitely open to serious offers as long as it's with the right director.' One such right director has been Julien Temple, who cast Koo as a girl taking part in a video marriage on BBC's *Arena*. 'It's a cameo role.'

BUBBLIN' DUBLIN

getting frisky on Irish Whiskey

Thanks to the bomb in Regent's Park there was scarcely an English face to be glimpsed at the Dublin Horse Show this year. The ball at the Burlington Hotel in aid of the Irish Epilepsy Association was equally short on what the tourist board described as 'notables'. Instead, credit-card supremos and deputy police commissioners whirled their wives round the dance floor to a keening rendition of 'I've Got You Under My Skin'. Even the horse put its foot down and refused to be auctioned. He finally went for a mere £800, less than half last year's figure. 'Let's be honest, all the quality have left Dublin anyway,' the barman told me. 'What you've got now with the money is a race of get-ups,' which when pressed to explain he defined as 'big fat people who order champagne for breakfast, the types you used to say "fully booked" to when they rang up for a table.' The horse agreed.

There are, of course, historical explanations. 'You have to understand that Ireland missed out on the three Rs,' one aristocratic survivor explained. 'The Romans, the Reformation and the Industrial Revolution.' More vexing still was the introduction of the wealth tax in 1974.

'I remember it was eight o'clock in the morning when my father rang me in London to tell me about the tax,' the 31-year-old Earl of Mount Charles told me. 'I'd been working at Faber & Faber and was just about to accept a job with the literary agent Hilary Rubinstein. My wife was eight months pregnant. I flew straight to Dublin and we spent three hours each wrestling with the lawyers and accountants. By the end of it my father had made Slane Castle over to me and decided to take himself off to the Isle of Man. It was a traumatic day.'

Pile after pile has gone under the hammer. Auction houses are having an Irish field day. This year already Adare Manor in County Limerick, ancestral home of the Earl and Countess of Dunraven, and Tulira Castle in County Galway, home of Lord and Lady Hemphill, have both been knocked down to the highest bidder. The Hemphills have been rehoused at a stud farm nearby, so that Lady Hemphill can still ride out as whipper-in with the Galway Blazers.

Perhaps it is no wonder that Lord Mount Charles is now Sotheby's Irish man on the spot and the Knight of Glin keeps his eyes peeled for Christie's.

But what of the famous tax exemption for creative writers? Alas, it has not brought about the Irish literary renaissance. It was an admirable scheme, but few serious literary figures enjoy the high tax bracket that makes them want to arise and go now and go to Innisfree, and the paperback millionaire who does have the incentive finds the Irish telephone system places a severe strain on his relationship with his agent. J.P. Donleavy stayed but Evelyn Anthony and Frederick Forsyth both gave up in the end, preferring the English limelight to the Celtic twilight. Gore Vidal bought and sold a small island near Bantry Bay. 'Nobody explained I'd have to live there,' he moaned. A bigger loss is Diana Mosley's son, the Hon Desmond Guinness, the dashing head of the Georgian Society. His house, Leixlip Castle, where he held a kind of court with his wife, the Württemberg Princess Marie-Gabrielle (Marega), became as much a social and cultural beacon as Harold Acton's house in Florence. Now they live apart. Marega keeps a melancholy vigil over Leixlip's social legend and Desmond, though he visits often, spends more and more time in London.

Meanwhile, the get-ups have been busy tearing down old Dublin. The Russell Hotel has been demolished. Trust House Forte got their hands on the Royal Hibernian. The Shelbourne flaunts a hideous new bar, the Gresham ominously awaits 'further modernisation'. A terrible beefburger is born.

Where do the 'notables' go at night? Snaffles in Lower Leeson Street is the best restaurant. Here you might see Sybil Connolly, the petite dress and fabric designer, on an outing from her smart little house in Merrion Square, chirruping away about sweet departed friends. Or Kieran Guinness brandishing his bubble-cut at a circle of London young.

Get-ups, on the other hand, flock to the sea-front Mirabeau, where the patron's Rolls-Royce outside establishes it as a place of tone. Inside, waiters procession past to music from *Swan Lake*, bowing and bearing aloft the dishes of the day, including a lobster which on its sixth encore seems to semaphore for help.

Those titled folk who have decided that Ireland will pull through live inevitably an eccentric existence. The inflationary cost of staff has boiled down every household to the barest tweeny. More often there is no tweeny or butler at all. At Slane Castle, a hefty lunch of wiener schnitzel and crème brûlée was served by an elfin youth in a maroon preppy blazer and winkle-pickers who dismissed himself with 'See ya!' when the coffee had been and gone.

Over in Westmeath, Thomas Pakenham is toughing it out at Tullynally Castle, and in Limerick the naughty Knight of Glin is fiercely protecting his flying staircase. The Earl of Rosse, Lord Snowdon's half-brother, at Birr Castle is fighting a rearguard action against the exorbitant upkeep of his woodland gardens. The strain of it all seems to be telling somewhat. He likes now to be known as Brendan rather than William and even adopts a strong Irish brogue when waving unexpected guests away to admire his eucryphia. Refusing to give up, too, are Sir Alfred and Lady Beit at Russborough, Lord and Lady Dunsany at Dunsany Castle, the Hon Garech Browne and Princess Purna at Luggala, and the Earl and Countess of Mount Charles at Slane Castle, all featured on the following pages. In effect, they are people living in a post-colonial situation. It's tempting to see them as characters in Irish versions of Paul Scott's Indian novels — O'Smalleys staying on.

The Beits

Sir Alfred and Lady Beit have had every provocation to abandon Ireland. In 1974 they were the victims of an IRA attack when Dr Bridget Rose Dugdale burst in and stole nineteen old masters. The experience has left some scars, but no bitterness against the Irish. Sir

Alfred becomes jumpy if he can't locate his wife in the house at any time, but it has done nothing to weaken their commitment to Russborough, the great Palladian monument they bought in 1952 to house their Rubenses, Gainsboroughs, Goyas and Vermeers.

The Beits are a distinguished-looking pair. Clementine is a Mitford — 'If I'd been a boy I would have been Lord Redesdale' — and she has their looks. Her hair is a gleaming silver meringue, her eyes autocratic cornflowers, her trim bosom encased in a Russborough souvenir T-shirt. After lunch she removes a thin cigar from an elegant silver case and smokes it through a tip-tilted cigarette-holder. Sir Alfred is sandy, tweedy and ironic. Nothing ridiculous escapes the gleam in his half-closed eyes.

It was his uncle, Alfred Beit, who made the family fortunes in South Africa. With Cecil Rhodes he founded the De Beers Diamond Company and used part of the fortune to acquire works of art, mainly pictures (Frans Hals's 'Lute Player', Vermeer's 'The Letter', Gainsborough's 'Italian Dancer', Goya's 'Doña Antonia Zarate') and Renaissance bronzes. Like his uncle, Sir Alfred Beit today has

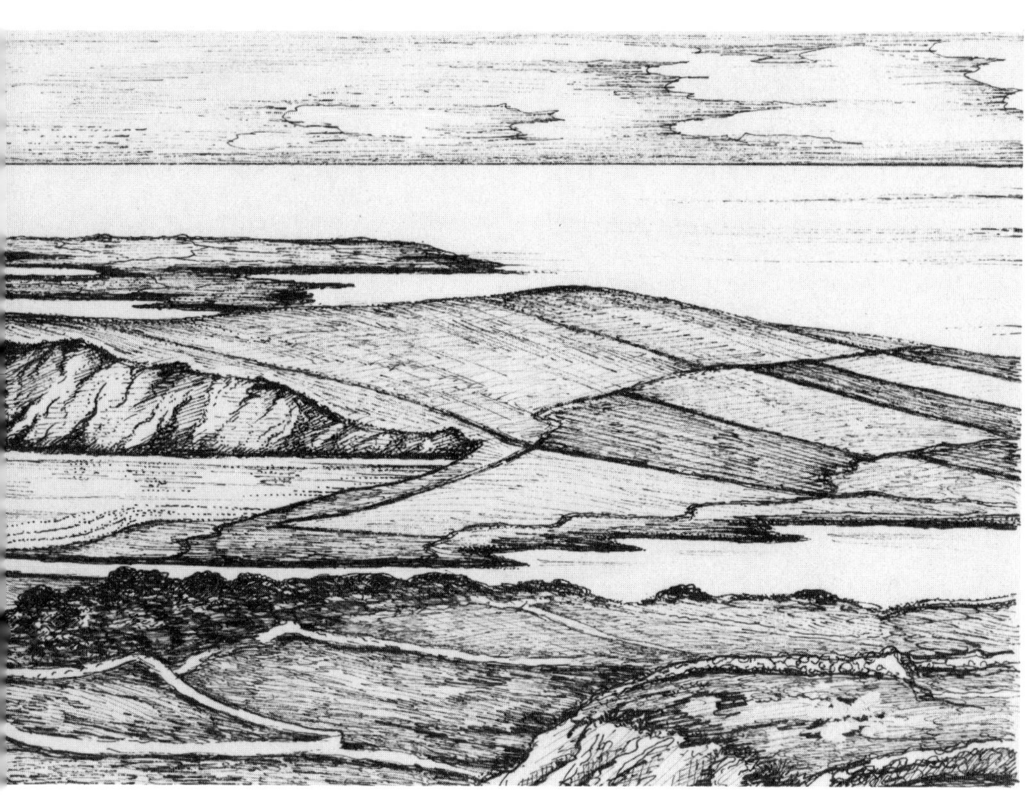

no heir and has turned the house and its contents over to the Alfred Beit Foundation, a body which has 'exceptionally strong trustees, the representatives of bona fide bodies, not just someone roped in for les yeux bleus'. The Beits rent their wing back from the Foundation.

Built in 1741 near Blessington in County Wicklow, the mottled granite of Russborough overlooks a lake the size of Windermere. Once it was the seat of the Earl of Milltown. Inside, the ceiling and staircases froth with exuberant stucco. The drawing-room has elaborately stuccoed walls as well. Plaster ovals were made expressly to show off the four Jospeh Vernet marine scenes that hang there now. Sir Alfred retrieved them from a New York stockbroker's flat, where they had ended up after Lady Turton unaccountably flogged them in 1926. 'Wasn't it unthinkable?' interjects Clementine. 'She absolutely didn't need the loot.'

Arts and music are Sir Alfred's passion. He is chairman of the Wexford Festival and always on the look-out for good singers. Russborough opens up for rare house-parties during Wexford fortnight, with such regular guests as John Julius Norwich, Lady Rupert Nevill, and Frank and Lady Kitty Giles. In his youth, Sir Alfred was a great traveller, making solo flights round Europe in the Thirties and canoeing up the Danube. He first spotted Russborough in *Country Life* in 1935, when he admired the fireplace in the dining-room and had it copied for his house in London. 'I didn't think much about it again until I saw it advertised in *Country Life* in 1951.' They had been living in South Africa where they still have a villa (Clementine: 'A bungalow, Alf') and found that 'the pictures fitted beautifully. Russborough had no real collection and it seemed their natural home.'

With hardly any staff, Russborough could be a lonely place in the evenings. A giant aerial on the roof is the rent they willingly pay for Radio Three. A baby goat nuzzling against the saloon window is at times the only company. Have they ever considered leaving since the IRA incident? 'Unthinkable,' said Clementine. 'There are too many things we love about Ireland. The people are so compassionate.'

'Yes, they're quite polite,' said Sir Alfred. 'And if we sold Russborough,' continued Clementine, 'it would all be broken up. You see, the new money sometimes likes to buy the houses but then their wives refuse to run them. They'd rather have a bungalow.' (Sir Alf: 'A villa, darling.')

The Mount Charleses at Slane

At Slane Castle Marquess Conyngham's son, the Earl of Mount Charles, is trying to stay cool about his unwieldy inheritance. He's put a night-club in the basement, opened a restaurant and kissed off the market-garden. ('OK, it's a bloody wilderness, but you can't beat your head against a brick wall for ever, can you?') He's also removed the woodburner from the Edwardian greenhouse to heat the house instead. ('Why should it only be warm in the night-club?') In July he pulled off a major coup by persuading the Rolling Stones to perform their penultimate concert at Slane. Seventy thousand fans turned up from north and south, a massive success, and in the early hours of the morning the Mount Charleses, Garech Browne and Jerry Hall joined hands and danced a jig. They're already working flat out on next year's bill.

At 31, Henry Mount Charles is as dashing as his Georgette Heyer name, with flowing ebony sideboards, a randy laugh, piercing grey eyes and bags of American slang. His navy blue Bentley is parked in the drive. 'A lot of leading figures are having to realise the ball-game's changed,' he told me. 'We in the south can't cast acquisitive eyes on the north. We have to build bridges not walls.' His wife, Juliet, is a tall, melon-mouthed blonde who talks in an attractive elongated drawl. They married against all parental wishes at twenty.

The main hall of the castle is a sea of children's tractors and puppy-chewed buckets and spades under the elk antlers and what Henry likes to call 'quite important' pictures. The drawing-room in the early morning is a lemon haze of battered damask. Paintings, busts and miniatures of George IV pop up everywhere to remind one that fat, fiftyish Lady Conyngham was the king's long-standing mistress. The ornate desk in front of the window was only one of his many gifts to her.

Slane Castle stands on a hill overlooking the River Boyne, a Gothicised Georgian cube. George IV is reported to have had the main road to Slane straightened to speed him on his journey to Lady Conyngham's bed. Returning here after a career at Harvard business school and then in publishing, Henry Mount Charles took some time to adjust. 'Now I consider myself managing director of a large company,' he told me. 'There's the upkeep of the house — a bottomless pit — my Sotheby's interest, the interior-design business that Juliet helps with, the night-club, the restaurant and now these concert deals. Believe me, every son-of-a-bitch with a house wanted the Stones, including the Guinnesses.' He seems slightly embarrassed about his more traditional activities — he shoots (he has a syndicate), he *used* to ride, he's involved in bloodstock. 'I can cope with any amount of hassle as long as Slane doesn't become a museum.' As he spoke, portable lavatories rolled up for use at a ceilidh for the disabled.

He is profoundly critical of the Haughey government, who 'don't give a damn about the heritage', and of the IRA, 'who represent nobody', and he is depressed by the number of his contemporaries who are forced to leave Ireland.

'A lot go to Australia. A lot to the US. Sometimes I'm tempted to go back myself. But you know, when I go to England I start to feel very Irish, even though it's obvious one is persona non grata since the bombings. Life in Ireland is so much more gregarious, and relaxed. You get a better social mix. When I go to dinner parties in Gloucestershire I can't believe the drivel I hear. My father said to me when he left for the Isle of Man, "Look, give it five years. I won't blame you if you give up." Well, five years have gone and I'm still here. And by God, if I've got to be the last living soul in a place like this, I'll be the last.'

The Devonshires at Lismore

Lismore, in County Waterford, is one of the Duke of Devonshire's clutch of houses. It sits high on the rocks above the River Blackwater, which is packed with salmon and trout. The Duke comes to Ireland every year for six weeks' fishing. In the Thirties the Duke's uncle, Charlie Cavendish, lived there with his wife Adéle, Fred Astaire's sister. He died in 1944, but Adéle returned to Lismore every summer until her own death in 1981. The hymn choice at her memorial service, 'A Pretty Girl is Like a Melody', reduced all Dublin society to tears. At Lismore today, the Duchess of Devonshire's magic touch is everywhere. The Victorian Gothic furniture was made by estate workers, and its slight shabbiness contributes to the poignant atmosphere of the house. The Duke has said of the setting, if any house had to go, Lismore would be the last.

The Dunsanys at Dunsany

Meath is hunting country and Plunkett country, the Plunketts of Dunsany — though Aileen Plunket (one 't') did rush off to Rome to join in the fun when Sir Oliver Plunkett (two 't's) was beatified in 1975.

Randal Plunkett, the present Lord Dunsany, is the son of the famous poet. His wife, Sheila, is the last Philipps of Picton Castle and one of the largest landowners in Pembrokeshire. They are a grand, funny couple. She, a pale, imperious blonde. He, a speckled military Adonis often coated in snuff. He was with the Indian Armoured Corps (Lt-Col) with Montgomery's army during the North African Campaign. Now 77, he spends all his time farming.

He was just back from the Dublin Antiques Fair when we met him. After a few minutes of grave suspicion he threw back his shoulders and shouted, 'Look at this! Cavalry stance! Is this photograph for another robbers' guide? Tell 'em it's all in a box or in the bank. Sorry I'm dressed in farming clothes, but I always like to go to an antiques show without me cheque-book and looking scruffy. Ever heard of an author called Irving? He was being a shocking bore all the way home in me motor.'

Inside, Dunsany is rich in texture, cluttered with mementoes of a travelled life. Originally it was a medieval castle, restored about 1780

Rosie Boot's Guide to London Bachelors

Luis Sosa Basualdo

He plays polo with Prince Charles. He skis with George Hamilton. When he's in London his crash-pad is the Eaton Terrace home of multi-millionaire Sir Gordon White. With such a quiver of contacts the fact that Argentinian playboy Luis Sosa Basualdo is stony broke himself is not as relevant as it might be in this column. His marriage to heiress Lucy Pearson was only dissolved in 1979 and he received the last payment of Lord Cowdray's £200,000 kiss-off last November. Any girlfriend at the moment? 'I prefer to wear a very low profile,' comments Basualdo, with a debonair flash of South American gums, 'My private life is sacred.'

Basualdo, 34, was educated in Argentina and America. He spent two years at the university of Miami majoring in surfing. He went on to join an investment bank in New York and hang out at the Racquet Club. In 1972 he married Lucy Pearson. He took to spending every summer playing polo at Cowdray Park or Petworth with the Egremonts. In 1977 Prince Charles turned out for his team the Golden Eagles and Basualdo's social success was assured. Wales apparently enjoys his company and in particular his taste in girls, said to be better than his taste in polo ponies.

Despite recent financial embarrassment, Basualdo is continuing to keep himself in the style to which he's accustomed. He has retained his New York apartment and a week-end house on Long Island. He buys his shoes at Lobbs, his shirts (silk) at Turnbull & Asser and his suits are tailor-made at Kilgour Weatherill. English girlfriends say that his preposterous elegance is redeemed by stunning performances on the polo field (he is a six-handicap player) and his willingness to go on to gamble at Aspinalls whatever the state of his bank balance.

You may ask what this light-footed Latin is doing in a guide which specialises in holding up for inspection the most desirable sprigs of nobility. I can only refer you to the wisdom contained in that famous song: 'I danced with a man who danced with a girl who danced with the Prince of Wales.'

and altered in the 1830s. The library is a red-red brown clutter with twin desks at either end, facing out at a misty green view. Lady Dunsany works strenously for local charities and heritage bodies. She even gets the breakfast in the morning. The days of the butler, footmen, maids and cooks are all gone, but Saint Oliver's ring is much in demand for miracles.

The Brownes at Luggala

'I reached the summit of the mountain above the magnificent valley and lake of Luggala,' wrote a traveller in 1829. 'The sun gilded all the country beneath me though the tops of the hills were yet shrouded in mist. It is indeed a lovely spot of earth, lonely and secluded; the wood full of game, the lake full of fish and nature full of poetry.'

The policeman put it another way: 'Keep on going, till you get to heaven.'

Luggala is a Regency Gothic pavilion in the Wicklow mountains, restored brick for brick by Garech Browne and his mother, Oonagh, when it was burnt down in 1957. Only the mantelpieces are now different. Today Garech lives here with his beautiful Indian wife, Princess Purna of Morvi, and a changing cast of raucous house guests.

He is a cuddly, anarchic figure with charismatic blue eyes and a light gold pony-tail. His wife prances around in a knee-length T-shirt with a glass of wine in one hand and a Chinese meat cleaver in the other. Inside, curry is prepared by a beetroot-faced novelist, Gerald Hanley, who announces every five minutes until midnight that the rice is just coming to the boil. But dishes are all mysteriously washed up by a picturesque OAP who wanders the corridors, on vacation from an old folks' home. When holiday-time comes she checks herself out and spends a fortnight working for Garech as she did in her youth, disappearing as secretively as she arrived. The wait for dinner becomes very suspenseful. Garech copes by racing off to do a pub-crawl in Roundwood with Viscount Gormanston's younger half-brother, Roderick O'Connor, a pale draculine young man of no fixed abode.

Most of Garech's conversation is dominated by his passing for the Chieftains, the band he signed up and launched in 1963, and a rediscovery of his bitterness against school: 'Boarding-school is not a training for life since nothing in life can ever be as remotely unpleasant again.'

Garech's hospitality at Luggala is warm, never-ending and very hard on the carpets. Cars drew up every half-hour disgorging fresh uninvited guests. The following day he was expecting Purna's mother's Indian chauffeur and his wife for a week. Sometimes, in the middle of all this action, Garech's big blue eyes become suddenly melancholy. 'Oh dear,' he says, 'can you remember what I've been piffling about?'

Rosie Boot's Guide to London Bachelors

The Hon J. Randle Siddeley

Just because the Hon J. Randle Siddeley is a landscape gardener it doesn't make him a nancy boy. On the contrary, he has a macho commitment to business and a penchant for very glamorous girls. If he slips out of Annabel's at midnight it means he's stressed rather than bored, since he's up at 6 a.m. every morning toting compost and making house calls on Belgravia's community of overtired *ficus elasticus*.

Siddeley, 26, is the eldest son of the celebrated interior designer, Lord Kenilworth. He is a spruce; together young man with a loud whinnying laugh and a springy head of perpendicular hair. He looks like the archetypal Hooray Henry but prides himself on being gritty. He had an undistinguished public-school career which culminated in his flunking out of the London College of Furniture and joining his father's firm. Within two years, as he is fond of saying, he had 'gone it alone', with his own gardening business planting prize-winning window boxes and doing a brisk trade in Arab patios. The way to his heart is to marvel at his career drive. 'I'm a perfect example of there being no reason to pass exams,' is a J. Randle refrain. 'It's all to do with personality and experience and the values you were brought up with. If my father had given me pocket money I wouldn't be the man I am today.'

The roots of Randle's drive may lie in the fact that Kenilworth Castle in Warwickshire is now a picturesque ruin. He lives in a converted warehouse in Blackfriars dominated by the tracks of his electric trains. Friends say that his egalitarianism weakens in the face of a buck's fizz when the overdog reasserts itself and he drops the line about not believing in hereditary peers. Nontheless, his circle are people who 'do things', even if they are not quite from the right side of the tracks.

He is traditionally careful about money but he is a generous and enthusiastic host with no time for wallflowers. Au fond, he has a well-defined sense of Them and Us. With a little gentle digging he may reveal buried treasure but don't over-water him. J. Randle Siddeley is no fool, and besides, as he is also fond of saying, if he'd been taught to believe in flattery he wouldn't be the man he is today.

WHAT A DENEUVE

Catherine by Bailey

She was always formidably self-possessed, but since the success of *The Last Metro* Catherine Deneuve is more in control than ever. Shared taxis stop at her destination first. Parties break up the moment she wants to leave. When her dinner escort, Serge Gainsbourg, embarks on a long chaotic anecdote she suddenly shouts, 'Follow that man!' 'Which man?' asks Gainsbourg, gazing bemusedly round Fouquet's. 'Your point!' cries Deneuve. 'I am trying to follow your point!'

Her vivacity comes as a surprise after years of reading about her 'frozen elegance', but then on this particular evening in Paris Deneuve is among friends — her ex-husband David Bailey, and Serge Gainsbourg, taking an evening off from his oriental girlfriend, Bamboo. Gainsbourg seems to enjoy the role of a joke figure in her life. He has currently become obsessed with a lurid murder case in which a Japanese student ate his girlfriend. 'You better be careful Bamboo doesn't eat you,' says Deneuve. She and Gainsbourg have a working partnership. She has just recorded a hit record with him, 'Remember to Forget Me'. 'That's my song,' Bailey says. 'It's everybody's song, darling,' says Catherine Deneuve.

The dinner is at the end of a long day. — filming with Yves Montand at Clichy until 5.30 and photographing with Bailey until 9.30 at the Clic Clac studios in Rue Daguerre, but Deneuve shows no signs of flagging. She had been an hour late for the session but only because of the rush-hour traffic. Whe she finally turned up no one recognised her at first. In her pink Saint Laurent mac she looked like the Avon lady, unexpectedly small and jaunty with mischievous mercantile brown eyes. Not until her long honey-coloured hair — darker now than it was, to make her look younger — was combed out into its familiar lion's mane did the film star begin to emerge. At 37, her figure retains its tautness. She only wears Saint Laurent and, contemptuous of a bra, chose a transparent beaded blouse that

Rosie Boot's Guide to London Bachelors

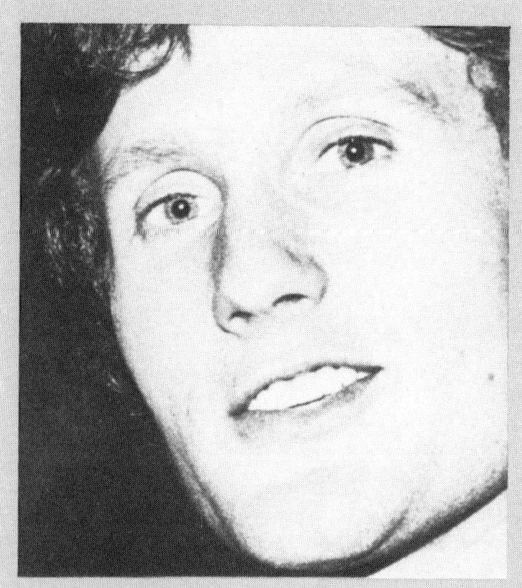

Sebastian Taylor

It's still possible to be fooled by Sebastian Taylor. Since he invested his backgammon wins in gold, he's even more popular. When he's in London he can be found any night of the week at the Clermont Club, shuffling and re-dealing his invitations. The first hint of commitment finds him hurtling for the airport. 'Jet planes are very good for one's love life. One either pretends one's just leaving or just arrived. This is why I get internationally good receptions.'

In social terms Taylor, 27, is a wholly self-invented figure. He is the son of academic doctors who brain-drained off to California when Sebastian left his prep school, the Dragon. He went to an American high school and Stanford University and returned to England with a scholarship in Law to Magdalen College Oxford. Here he switched to English and teamed up with a blow-dried smoothie called Patrick Donovan (now prematurely middle-aged and in banking) and hung about with the Park Town Set (Adam Carr, Lord Neidpath, Nick Ashley) looking cool and quoting Keats' *Eve of St Agnes*. His patina of literacy is still impressive to Brazilians and Arabs.

Since Oxford, Sebastian has been an international house-guest, living on his wits. He's got most of his mileage out of his Shelleyan curls and his gift for wild self-parody which ossified somewhere along the line and left him with the vaulting vowels of a Jane Austen cad. He finds everything 'To-tally ridiculous'.

'I set out to defy the natural law in England and make some money,' he announced when I paged him in the V.I.P. lounge at Heathrow on his way to speculate for oil in Texas. 'I have made an enormous BARREL of money and I intend to spend it wildly, lavishly. How I made it is shrouded in secrecy. Suffice it to say I won half a million at backgammon and played the commodity market like a dream. The gold market has been exceedingly kind to me. My newest venture is spudding wells in Texas, and I now know better than Robert Anderson the difference between a gusher and a moonshot. I'm also giving greater consideration to marrying big money. I am currently going out with a ravishingly beautiful Arab princess and I'm quite prepared to be circumcised if necessary.'

In fact, Taylor could never pay the rent for marrying money. He is a social mountaineer who wants to leave his own visiting card on Mount Olympus. He has only been in love once, with Clio Goldsmith, and he dreads reciprocation. His contemptuous charm makes him a great hit with masochistic women who interpret his aloofness as playing hard to get — a bad mistake. This Mr Darcy never melts in the last reel.

showed a glimpse of fist-like breasts and youthful neck.

Between photographs she pulled on a cigarette, swung her legs and broke into occasional heartless snatches of song. Critics praising her performance in *The Last Metro* have likened Deneuve to Grace Kelly. Truffaut has indeed extracted rare depths from her usually glacial surface and put her, after 40 films, into the legend league. Her new screen image — creamy, wise, inaccessible but brimming with sexual mystery — brilliantly defies her gossip-column life as the whirlwind wife of Bailey and the mother of two illegitimate children by Roger Vadim and Marcello Mastroianni.

It is far removed, too, from her almost hoydenish social personality. How did she do it? She looks irritated. 'I don't like people who make a fuss about how they did something,' she says. 'I like to laugh and joke on the set and then when the director says go, I just do it.' She turns to Gainsbourg, who, refreshed by a bullshot, has resumed his shaggy-dog story. 'Bored by his interminable story our heroine slew him at last with a toothpick,' she says, giving a tiny stab to his elbow. Then she calls for the bill (paid by the radio station who do a nightly broadcast from Fouquet's — Serge and Catherine had done their three minutes between courses), gives a quick dazzling smile to the boss of a cosmetics firm at the next table, a short, urgent demand to the PR man of the record company to dive across the street to an all-night drugstore and supply me with her new LP, and heads for the exit.

'Have you got one franc for the toilette?' says Bailey. 'I've only got ten francs,' says Deneuve. 'We'll go together and split it.' The French Grace Kelly keeps her royalty firmly for the screen.

APRIL ASHLEY NOW

When I met April Ashley she was feeling very proud. She had just returned from a holiday in Florida, where a one-night whirl with a 25-year-old beach boy had turned into a two-week affair. 'It was the first time in *years* a lover hadn't known about my past,' she told me. 'I kept thinking, "Shall I or shan't I?" Then I thought, "No. I'll send him the book instead".'

The book (*April Ashley's Odyssey*, Jonathan Cape) when it arrives, will put a new complexion on the beach boy's holiday romance. He will discover, for a start, that his lover was once a man.

Born George Jamieson, a sailor's son and one of nine children (not all of whom lived), April Ashley grew up in the slums of Liverpool where 'the only night life was being beaten up and murdered'. She spent her schooldays being bullied for looking effeminate ('Run? I was the fastest runner in the school!') and sped into the unlikely haven of the Royal Navy. Life aboard the *Pacific Fortune* was no picnic. In naval uniform April looked 'like a vaudeville act'. During those voyages to Jamaica and the Panama Canal she was hassled and jeered into two suicide attempts, and then, on discharge, she drifted up to London for more Grand Guignol misery.

She was a table-wiper at a Lyon's Corner House, eating benzedrine, wearing green eyeshadow and later mixing with a squad of screeching freaks and misfits who were always trying to kill themselves and spoke in a strange patois of their own ('Have another popper, daddyo, and shut your eke'). The turning point was an audition to be a female impersonator at Le Carrousel in Paris, where

she encountered, for the first time, the sophisticated end of drag. The other performers were all exotic basket-cases living in the penumbra of indeterminate sex. There was Bambi, Capucine and Peki d'Oslo, otherwise Alain Tapp, nowadays Amanda Lear. Above all there was Coccinelle — he who'd had five nose jobs, an ear job, a face-lift and silicone breasts implanted and who blazed the trail with a sex change.

Inspired, our heroine set off to Casablanca and the climax of her life's escape — the exciting Dr Burou. It was his wizard surgery that finally turned George Jamieson into April Ashley and dispatched her back to Paris with all the female machinery — a first-class 'zee zee' technically competent to fool in the dark any but the most discerning beach boy.

'Can you imagine how I felt? I had become this ravishing creature and believe me I was reaching for the *stars*. Nothing was going to stop me from having it *all*.' For a time she did. She made a wild entrée into high society in London, whooped it up with Sarah Churchill and Peter O'Toole and married the Chief Scout's son, the Hon Arthur Corbett, now Lord Rowallan, for whom she was the fulfilment of a lifetime of repressed transvestite fantasy. But she left him in Marbella and the marriage ended in acrimonious divorce in 1970. The judge's summing up was a cruel reward for April's vale of jeers. 'I hold, that it has been established that the respondent is not and was not, a woman at the date of marriage, but was at all times a male.'

'My lawyer,' she murmurs now, 'was wiped off the floor by Arthur's. My golly, Tina, if you ever want a divorce, Joe Jackson is your man. He'll get you pots of money and make you out a *virgin*. But no, I'm not bitter for myself so much as for all those other poor transsexuals who can never be legally married. Just because Arthur and I made such a farcical mess of things it doesn't mean it couldn't have worked between two other people. Of course there are hundreds of transsexuals living quietly as wives — look at Amanda Lear, she's married a French film director — but now because of my legal precedent they have to live in terror that one day the men who pardoned them will turn. That seems terribly unfair.'

At 44 April has a strange, startled presence that causes passers-by to stare. Her style is lodged in the early Sixties — there are shades of beatniks in the old sweater and Mandy Rice-Davies in the bleached bouffant hair. Her face has a sweet blank look to it. Her head nods like Little Weed. Her voice husks away like an ageing duchess who's lived for the last ten years on whisky sours. Since her divorce she has drifted about the world falling in and out of love, running a restaurant for three years in Egerton Garden Mews and conquering the jeunesse dorée at Oxford. Now, after two heart attacks, she lives alone, pottering around with Flora, the dog, in a nine-roomed house left to her by an elderly neighbour in Hay. Occasionally she comes up to London, stays with friends — usually young men — and sees old chums like Anton Dolin. Defying doctor's orders, she'll turn up at Tramp and sit alone at the bar, chatting. 'I drink. I'm a tremendous drunk.'

She believes a permanent relationship is impossible for her. The love of her life was a young student, Edward Madok, who died in a car crash when their affair was already over. 'People are so cruel. At first Edward adored the celebrity of being linked with me. Then he hated being introduced as April Ashley's boyfriend. I suppose if I'd been sensible I would have stayed married to Arthur because he did adore me so. The trouble was, I was never in love with him. I was constantly unfaithful. He used to say to me, "April, I have enough love for two," and I would say, "But *Arthur*, I have to love too." You see, I'd put up with bullshit all my life and after my operation I felt so strong and triumphant. I had all the arrogance of youth. I suppose if I'd known what I know now I wouldn't have been so cocky. On the other hand, the lows I've experienced are only of the same proportion as the tremendous highs.'

She claims she learnt not to cry in the Navy. 'I knew I had to keep it all in or I'd be beaten up. It was very frightening. I had this certainty planted in my brain at my birth, perhaps before my birth, that I am a woman, but I had no one to speak about it to. It wasn't until I read Christine Jorgensen's story in the papers that I realised I was not the only freak in the world.'

Her deepest low seems to have been the wake of her divorce when her pre-operative self was exposed in every trashy newspaper. 'Suddenly I had become this act — April Ashley. A celebrity by night. Unemployable by day. I couldn't even get a job as a salesgirl. I had people sticking their fingers into my tits to see if they were real. Which they were of course — I had spontaneous breast growth right from the word go *and* a seventeen-inch waist. But I am a shy person at heart and it all became unbearable.'

Her greatest highs were and continue to be the joys of her womanhood. Her twenty-year on-off affair with 'Joey', a married man who never really appreciated her, her whirlwind romance with a young Spanish aristocrat for whom she ran away from Arthur, and her recent triumph in America. 'Pulling that boy in Florida recently was a high. There were all these gorgeous creatures around me and he preferred *me*. It wasn't just sex. He liked my conversation. Who *cares* about Women's Lib? I just want to fall into a man's arms and

Rosie Boot's Guide to London Bachelors

Patrick Rattray

Don't slap Patrick Rattray's face when he tells you he's a clan chieftain's son in his own counry. The fact that he looks as if he's climbed out of a sock is no reflection on his pedigree. Nor is it a clue to his finances that he pays for a croissant at the Little Chef on his American Express card. 'The point about Paddy,' a friend says, 'is that he wouldn't spend any money even if he had any.' It doesn't matter; it seems that cash is apparently not the basis for Paddy Rattray's legendary sexual success.

He was born in 1947, the eldest son of Major Rattray of Rattray and Christian Guthrie of Guthrie and heir to Craighall-Rattray, a family pile perched 200 feet above the river Erricht in Perth. He was sent to Harrow and Edinburgh University where he read geology and became a very late flower child, hanging out in New York and the pub at Blair Gowrie. His mother died when he was sixteen and he and his sisters were taken under the wing of Sir Iain Moncreiffe of that Ilk, the highly sexed heraldry freak who writes for *Books and Bookmen.*

When Paddy was 27 his father went off to live in Spain with his second wife, Elizabeth, the daughter of Lord De L'Isle, and made over Craighall to his eldest son who resourcefully divided it up into holiday flats and let it out to kidnap-fleeing Italian jet setters. He now lives in Camden, a brillo-haired Lothario, biding his time till the day when he'll be entitled to wear three feathers in his Tam o'Shanter at the Caledonian Ball.

If you like your beaux adventurous, Paddy Rattray is your man, willing at the drop of a hat to whisk you down to the Caledonian stand-by queue at Heathrow and take you away to see his hereditary heather. He is a man of few words, but all of them are jokes — and he does a very good impersonation of Miss Jean Brodie.

forget about it all. Today was a high too. That nice photographer. All those beautiful clothes. This lunch. I shall start to enjoy it when I think about it at home.'

Why is April rushing into hard covers? Inevitably, she is rather broke, despite the house in Hay. 'I've never thought poor. I'm afraid I'm a terrible Scarlett O'Hara, always believing in tomorrow.' It seems she had been trying to persuade Duncan Fallowell, a journalist friend she has known since his undergraduate days at Oxford, to write her story for thirteen years. He agreed to do so finally when his career hit a major snag with the collapse of Baron Stephen Bentinck's magazine, *Boulevard*, of which he was a leading light. April herself had scrawled a boxful of notes when her last heart attack kept her bedridden for three months, but what Fallowell produced from these and the hours and weeks with the tape-recorder is far from a ghost-writing job. *April Ashley's Odyssey* is a New Journalism novel, a camp *Tristram Shandy* that captures all the vitality of its subject's personality but provides at the same time an interpretive alibi for her life.

'The transsexual's dream,' he has her saying, 'is to become a normal man or woman. This is not possible through surgery. Transsexuals should not delude themselves on this score. If they do, they are letting themselves in for a big, possibly lethal disappointment. It is important they should understand themselves as *transsexuals* and if they find this difficult, various groups and associations are there to help them. It is all very civilised and chatty these days.'

April herself is brusque about any notion that she is now lonely or disappointed. The book is intended to be, above all, optimistic and confident, a valedictory V-sign to her origins. 'I wouldn't belittle April's suffering,' Duncan Fallowell said, 'but I think she's learnt to live with her sadness and keep it in its place. She was born into darkness and found her own way to the light when she went to Casablanca. Compared to that great achievement, sadness seems relatively trivial.'

THE GENTLEMAN HACK

those who grub in Grub Street

High Church Hugo is a gentleman hack. Please don't ever confuse him with a journalist. He is hostile to facts and even more hostile to investigation. His corner is very much the well-turned think-piece, or well-cobbled Cobbett, published once a week in a range of ailing literary and political organs.

He does quite a lucrative line in being cast against type — a football column which purports to know nothing about football. A restaurant column which returns again and again to an 'extremely agreeable trattoria' in Greek Street where the 'house red is as good as anything I've tasted in Provence'. Occasionally he likes to surprise his public with a burst of knowledgeability on an arcane subject. 'Did you know Hugo is very good on trees?' is the way his friends tend to discuss his political column. Indeed, barking up the wrong ones becomes more and more his trade-mark as he earns a small literary success.

Another of Hugo's professional trade-marks is his refusal to learn to type. His copy is always hand-written and submitted with an apologetic note to the editor's secretary. He yearns to be paid in guineas but since this is clearly impossible he contents himself with writing enthusiastic pieces about the new florin.

Although his prose style is 75, Hugo himself is only 38. Physically, he does his best to catch up. He walks with a literary stoop and pushes aside a rumpled hank of prematurely grey hair. His dress tries to denote the aristocratic reach-me-down tradition —

hence the goose-shit green corduroy trousers and deafening tweed jacket (acquired from the Dead Man's department) which he always teams with one of two detached collar shirts and a ferociously knotted polyester tie. The all-important country roots are suggested by a pair of lumpen brown brogues. The point of all this is to make self-made men feel over-dressed. 'I say, *you're* looking smart' is the way Hugo demoralises a dinner guest who arrives wearing a clean sweater and unstained trousers.

Despite his farm-yard feet, Hugo does not possess a country house himself. He relies on the weekend hospitality of a repertoire of rich school-friends. On these occasions he augments his wardrobe with a tartan dressing-gown and a decaying pigskin sponge-bag whose contents of athlete's foot powder, Senacot and Elastoplast are reconstructed from literary memories of the bathroom life of bachelor uncles.

The thing that Hugo yearns for you to say is that he's 'a sort of eighteenth-century figure'. After all, his theme is mankind even if his house is in Stockwell. And his life embodies great eighteenth-century traditions — bad skin, old suits and a black and white television.

One of the strongest themes in Hugo's weekly column is the enduring values of family life. Situation apart, Hugo does have a very nice house, if poorly heated. It is a Georgian workman's cottage with, as he puts it, 'relatively few Third World neighbours'. There are hunting prints in the hall. The lavatory seat is mahogany, and there are dog hairs, if no dog, on the battered green chesterfield. A false bell-cord hangs from the wall. Over the fireplace is a cracked portrait of a knowing Roundhead which Hugo likes to imply came from the attic of a 'grandish' cousin in Wiltshire. The drum table in front of the window groans under a stack of gentleman hack reading — fly-fishing manuals (there are many flies, if no fish, in Stockwell), old *Private Eyes* (Hugo informs on his editors' sex lives for a small retainer), a second-hand copy of Pope's *Epistle to Arbuthnot* and a 1968 edition of the *Guinness Book of Records*. Beside this is an expensive, glossy pile of recent publications. These are review copies of tree encyclopaedias that pause on the drum table before being flogged at the bookshop in Grape Street which gives Hugo 'a jolly good rate, all things considered'.

Perhaps the only fly in the domestic ointment is Hugo's family life. His wife Miranda is unexpectedly glamorous and moody. She is a spirited brunette with pretty eyes and bad legs and keeps Hugo on the hop with long bouts of mysterious umbrage. Often when he gets in she's on the phone speaking urgently in very good French. Once a month she specialises in creating social tension for Hugo by arriving an hour late for the theatre or suddenly speeding home in a taxi from the one cocktail party that will do his career good.

During the course of their fourteen-year-marriage Miranda has left Hugo twice. Once for a highly sexed architectural correspondent who got cold feet and sent her back, and once for a 22-year-old sculptor she met in a café on the way to cadge a holiday from Hugo's cousin in Antibes. Nowadays she doesn't leave Hugo but every so often kicks him out. On these occasions he goes and stays with his elder brother, a schoolteacher in Dorset, and pretends to be writing a book about the decline of the Whig Junto. What else can he do? Miranda is due to inherit a capacious rectory in Wales and all his friends think he's lucky. Meanwhile the unpredictability of her behaviour gives Hugo his daytime aura of vague, heterosexual dismay.

The other problem is his children. Eton was too expensive so Hugo decided to send them to what he always calls the 'village school' — the local comprehensive. This means that Emily, Willie and Charlie all speak with grating Cockney accents. In Hugo's column Charlie often has a precocious quibble about semantics and Emily is very funny about the new prayer book. Actually, when Hugo dismounts from his bicycle at 5.30 he finds them all slumped in front of the (colour) television or boorishly cut off by their Sony Walkmans. Ecclesiastical Emily's only real claim to Eccentricity is a coarse American T-shirt which reads 'Up your ass, Soldier Blue'.

This slogan especially pains Hugo because of his other slight marital problem. It is, I'm afraid, the legacy of public school, despite his column's strong ridicule of what he terms 'homosexualists'. He has, of course, done nothing much about it. Instead, he channels his feelings into misogynist solidarity with his friends like Gerry, a Radio Four producer who's very good on cheese; Henry, a pundit who's very good on fleas; and Freddie, a polemicist who's particularly good on knees. The three of them like to linger over the plonk

WHO'S
WHO
1982
BALZAC
Spectator

at El Vino's discussing bad backs, bouncing cheques and pushy women. About twice a year they review each other's books, usually a collection of old columns flung together under an Augustan title. Hugo recently reviewed Henry's *Immodest Proposals* in *Books and Bookmen*. 'In his earlier and wholly delightful volume Henry Blount introduced us to some of his ancestors,' his piece began. 'now in *Immodest Proposals* we have the even more agreeable experience of meeting some of his friends,' i.e. Hugo, Gerry and Freddie, who privately hold very different opinions about Henry's book.

'I must say, Henry's pieces don't really stand the test of time, do they?'

'Amazing really that he flogged the serial rights at all.'

'Yes, but apparently George only printed 500 copies.'

'Oh Lord, does Henry know?'

'Apparently not. He seemed *frightfully* cross this morning that he's not on an author tour of Scunthorpe.'

(Hopefully) 'I suppose Emily's giving him hell?'

'Apparently she's gone to stay with her mother.'

'*Poor* Henry.'

At these El Vino gatherings politics, too, are the subject of bibulous debate. Hugo, Gerry, Henry and Freddie are all high Tories as you would expect. This does not mean they are particularly keen on Mrs Thatcher (they preferred 'Peter' Carrington). Her grocery origins, like Ted Heath's (another bête noir), are too strenuously middle class. The Falkland Islands? They giggled a bit about this florid espisode in English history, managing to be both *for* and *against* the war. *For* winning but *against* all the middle-class land of hope and glory that went with it. Real spleen is reserved for an old grievance against Peter Walker. It was he who turned bits of Wiltshire and Gloucestershire into Avon. On foreign policy Hugo, Gerry, Freddie and Henry pursue a keenly individualist line. They are Arabists, but — very important — *old* Arabists (the PLO are far too sweaty), deriving their conviction from a wistful desire to dress up in a caftan and share a tent in the desert with a beautiful Bedouin boy. Being an Arabist is also a good excuse for being anti-Semitic. Economics? Fright-fully boring. They also pose a literary problem. There is not much under 'economics' in the *Oxford Book of Quotations*. The gentleman hack thinks Alec Douglas-Home was the best prime minister we ever had, but didn't stick for him when he was there.

In a dream situation, what does the gentleman hack want to be? Editor of *The Times* or Director-general of the BBC. But isn't ambition supposed to be uncouth? Unfortunately deep down the

Rosie Boot's Guide to London Bachelors

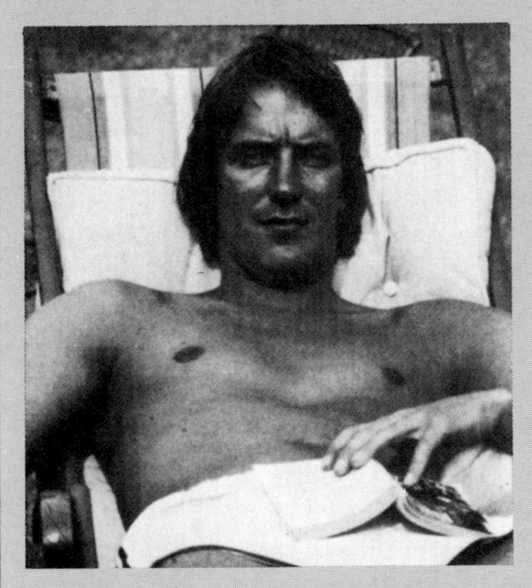

Mike Russell Hills

This one is really pretty, although you might not believe it from the photograph.

For a start, he's tall. Alone among the fleet of midgets hitherto featured in this column he stands six foot two inches without his motor-cycle boots. Then there is his pleasing (and deceptive) air of healthy living. Frequent trips abroad make him an agreeable honey colour all the year around. What then is the snag? Mike Russell Hills is that lethal genre of charmer — the one who can't stop himself.

His prospects, it seems, are rather good. He is a television commercial director who, at 33, has landed most of the plum clients. Saatchi give him the Conservative Party ad to do and his directorial touches caused a fetching blush to mantle the cheeks of Mrs Thatcher. (Don't tell Denis.) Schweppes, BP, British Leyland and British Caledonian all compete for his talents and in his time he's carried off most of the advertising trophies. He now has his own company, Reel to Reel, and operates out of an office in D'arblay Street. 'I couldn't work from home. Nobody takes an 874 telephone number seriously.' At night he hangs out with up-market ad-men at the Alibi, but he's a willing escort to premières — as long as you are starring in the film.

Which brings me to the worrying bit. Russell Hills has daunting standards when it comes to girlfriends. Since the age of fourteen he has never been seen with a dog. He tends to go for brand-name heiresses or Middle-European nobility and he always favours two distinct categories — the fey English rose and the exotic brunette. Added to this there is an astonishing repertoire of pass-through conquests whom he didn't mean to fall in love with him. At one point his lunch dates were regularly steered to a particular Chinese restaurant in the Fulham Road where the damp adoring gaze of a tiny waitress was always accompanied by a double portion of spring roll.

In an upwardly mobile mood last month he bought a palatial house on Clapham Common, but he seems in no hurry to share it. He is off to Australia for three weeks at Christmas to set up a commercial. When he gets back he'll be directing an English news programme for American TV.

Is he going to settle down? The *on dit* goes that he lives at a hectic pace. He keeps an oxygen spray beside his bed to revive himself after nights of wild excess, and its's my belief that the James Bond phase isn't over yet. He drives a black Porsche, a monstrous BMW and is even rumoured to have an Oriental dressing-gown behind locked cupboards. He also sleeps in an eye-mask which could make the sensitive girl feel like Tonto.

He's funny and smart and I did warn you — *very* pretty, but as to Mike Russell Hills and marriage, *quien sabe?*

gentleman hack is very, very ambitious, hence his hatred of meritocrats. Indeed he is possessed by a hard and desperate longing for money, rank and recognition. How can he achieve this and conserve his image of cordial irrelevance? It can be done. Take his hero, Archie, a literary critic who's very good on fees. A big noise on the Arts Council, the British Museum and the IBA, Archie is also rich. He married it (his father-in-law is an earl), so without the opprobrium of having to strive he owns a very large Georgian house in Wiltshire.

Archie's great career success is one long eighteenth-century bamboozle. While lesser gentleman hacks *are* hopeless about money, Archie *appears* to be hopeless about money. In reality he makes a packet on the stock exchange, acting on hot tips from Algy (very good on Belize), who writes the business column in a more prosperous weekly. While lesser gentleman hacks are trained to be hostile to personal publicity, Archie *appears* to be hostile. His greatest coup was managing to be the subject of a television profile which filmed him at mass. Afterwards he was filmed again writing his diary in black Italic script, as the voice-over told viewers, 'Archie Holman-Ross is, above all, a very *private* man.' And though, like all gentleman hacks, Archie's manner is genial to all, he is malicious towards most. His memory for slights goes well beyond the day when he failed to get into Pop at Eton. His new job with the IBA provides some satisfying moments. Through his bi-focals Archie's sententious gaze can pick out the bustling new local radio applicant and identify him twenty years later as the umpire who gave him LBW. 'I'm not sure about their line on profit sharing,' he begins at the meeting afterwards. And so, with a light churchman giggle, Archie puts the boot in.

Three cheers for the gentleman hack for keeping alive great eighteenth-century traditions! In the new Thatcher England his brand of idle libertarianism has never been safer. Where would we be without his weekly output of well-Cobbetted cobblers?

A Spotter's Guide to the Gentleman Hack

Likes
Wodehouse, Waugh, Anthony Powell (pronounced Pole), pyjamas, writing paper with pseudo Reynolds Stone device, baskerville type and V-shaped envelope folds, port, Victorian Narrative painting, Malcolm Mugggeridge, cricket, chain-smoking, bicycles (to turn London into Oxford), big slobbering dogs, Victorian sing-songs, half-hunters or other anachronistic dress details, fountain pens, Kipling, Kingsmill, Poe (*old* drugs), coarse-cut marmalade (coarser than Benny Hill), nostril hair, razor nicks, the Reverend Edward Norman, old telephone codes (TATe Gallery 1234), cheese shops, chesterfields, train-journeys, Trollope, toffees, turn-ups.

Watering-holes (many) **& eating-houses** (few) El Vino's, the Duke of York's, the French Pub, Zanzibar. (They *miss* Muriel's.) The Venus Kebab House and Bertorelli's in Charlotte Street; Gay Hussar, Boulestin, Escargot (when someone else is paying).

Killing time
The London Library, the Reading Room of the British Museum, Vermilion Books in Red Lion Street, Patisserie Valerie, the RAC's Turkish bath, Music Discount in Rathbone Place for knock-off Wagner

Chez eux
Shabby leather-bound books in sets, Izal lavatory-paper in baskets, framed cartoons, planters full of ash and spiders (no plants), moth-eaten Persian runners, inherited Bakelite wirelesses, anything that 'came with the house', architectural and topographical prints, the odd shocking knockdown piece from Times Furnishing or MFI.

Table d'hôte
Soupe à l'oignon with yesterday's baguette à l'ail, rognons de boeuf au riz (one ox kidney feeds eight), Brie from the deli and a fresh baguette, café filtre from the Algerian Coffee House in Old Compton Street (dripped into Provençal earthenware), vin rouge Corbières.

Holidays
Tuscany, the Massif Central, Salzburg (on a freebie), Cornwall, the Rhôné Valley (on a freebie), Bayreuth (*next* year), Andorra (to stay with step-mother-in-law), Venice out of season at a pensione on the Zattere ('where Ruskin lived'), fishing in Scotland.

Cars
Anything rusted up to L-registered.

Hates
TV, foreigners, electric typewriters, homosexuals, seat-belts, the *Sunday Times*, psychiatrists, muesli, motorbikes, Melvyn Bragg, architects, after-shave, abstract arts, D.H. Lawrence, joggers, investigative journalism, duvets, digital clocks, real haircuts, photography, paperbacks, cremation, contraception, Clive James, the Barbican, pre-sliced bacon, Edward Heath, Channel Four.

LIFE AS A PARTY

the life and death of a gossip columnist

There are no parties for Timothy Swallow to go to this year. Not the kind at which he used to star and have his epigrams written up — often by himself — in a rash of fly-by-night magazines. Remember *Boulevard, Frizz, London Index, Gold*? The magazines are dead and so is Timothy Swallow. London now lacks the energy to re-invent him.

He was tiny, like an exotic fly with shiny hair, darting nose and sparkling, malicious eyes. For five years he whirred around on the fringe of fame bringing to it a trashy iridescence. Wherever there was a free sausage or a glass of champagne he would buzz down, circle each group and immortalise it with his sting. He was a star-maker for the also-rans, a Boswell for the B-list, who slipped out into the Fleet Street mainstream and drowned. He was a child of the gossip age, Nigel Dempster's dead heir.

Fame as an infection incubates well 120 miles north of London. Timothy Swallow was born in 1955 in Gainsborough, Lincolnshire, the eldest son of Kenneth and Beryl Swallow. In 1959 the Swallows moved to a pleasant road in Doncaster, to a small, angular house they were constantly doing up. Timothy was always keenly aware that the only glamour puss to come out of Doncaster was Kevin Keegan.

For the past twenty years his father, Kenneth Swallow, has been in charge of the drawing office at ICI fibres. Beryl Swallow works as a clerk for an engineering firm. Jeffrey Swallow, Timothy's younger brother, is the catering manager at Little Plumstead Hospital in

Norwich. All three Swallows resemble straight versions of Timothy. Jeffrey and Kenneth both have the rounded, copious hair of his pre-punk days while Beryl has his smallness and speed.

Timothy went to Doncaster Grammar School. He was the last to take the 11-plus before the education system changed. He was a high flier at English, a star in the school plays, but was bored by Maths and came home spotless after rugger. Films were his obsession, and autobiographies. He kept a diary of who had starred in all the films he'd seen. While Jeffrey read football magazines, Timothy became a challenge to Doncaster library's showbusiness section. He polished an impersonation of Bette Davis. 'Going to the pictures with him was always an event,' his mother said. 'If it was a horror film he'd scream. If it was a comedy he'd laugh out loud. We used to say, "Don't show yourself up" — but he didn't care. After the film he'd always want to analyse the performance. Apparently Kenneth and I missed the whole point of *Apocalypse Now*.'

He was always clearly different. A 'one off', as his mother puts it, 'one out of the blue'. Unlike the rest of the family, for instance, he never acquired a Yorkshire accent. Later, when he became a gossip columnist, his voice became an important asset — mellifluous, intimate, exuding a classless courtesy, it broke down the barriers of the frostiest adulterer. He had sprung from the womb with perfect diction. 'Timothy's mind was not Doncaster,' his father explains it. 'London was always his Mecca. He was cracked on it. We were brought up to keep our noses to the grindstone, get a pension at the end of it. Not Timothy. He used to say, "Somebody's got to have it" — the limelight. I don't know where he got his flamboyancy.'

'When he was going to the station he used to order these mini-cabs then lie in the bath,' his mother said. 'I used to say, "Timothy, hurry up, your taxi's here." And he always said the same thing — "LET HIM WAIT". And do you know, they always did.'

'He used to run up enormous phone bills,' Kenneth Swallow added. 'Money and Timothy were not compatible.'

Timothy left Doncaster Grammar School and went straight to London. He had flirted with a diploma course in TV journalism at a London polytechnic then changed his mind. The local paper didn't interest him either. He was going to by-pass craft. He rented a room in Albert Road, Battersea, from a landlady recommended by a

Doncaster parson. Wearing the navy and white pin-striped suit his mother had bought him, he got a job in Peter Jones's china and glass department, and quelled his longings for social stardom by becoming the life and soul of the church group at St Mary's, Bourne.

He re-met an old school friend, Jane Polden, who was now reading Law at Cambridge, where Timothy started to spend weekends. It was a platonic relationship. Jane is a lanky redhead with reckless eyes and a tendency to bursts of immoderate laughter. She shared his idea of himself. 'We used to talk and talk and have fantasies together, always based on him being famous. Gore Vidal loomed large in his life. We knew the first paragraph of *Myra Breckinridge* off by heart!' He became obsessed by David Bowie and started to wear mascara. 'After the kiss, the make-up,' he used to say as he applied it.

In the midst of this hectic self-creation he decided to get confirmed. He seemed to hang on to his religious streak through all the later costume changes. Even though his dress, demeanour and prose were a series of wild hints he never declared himself a homosexual. If he'd wished to leap from the closet the circles he mixed in later would have welcomed it and even his parents might have been relieved to see him settled at last as an honest-to-god pansy. But he never did, pushing on perhaps for the moment of celebrity that would transcend the confusion of sex.

In Doncaster Beryl Swallow worried about her son, but she never doubted the symbolism of London in his life. North and South, as far as the Swallows were concerned, were divided by a behavioural chasm Inter-city couldn't bridge. They viewed anything that happened there through a moral telescope, gratified to be excluded. When Jeffrey arrived to stay with Timothy after a three-week weight-lifting course at Tonbridge Wells, what appalled him was not the mascara but the fact that Timothy 'hadn't bought a thing for tea.'

But Timothy was shedding the mores of Doncaster fast. He gave up his job at Peter Jones and went for the more glamorous aroma of selling advertising space for Scottish TV. He started to tire of his bedsitter and took to booking himself in for refreshing bouts of luxury at the Inter-Continental Hotel. If he saw a jacket or a sweater he liked, he just bought it, irrespective of the price. Then something happened — a loss of control. He ran up a bill for £1,000 in Harrods

and tried to cut his wrists at a Chelsea hotel.

His parents took him back in Doncaster. There, he sat in his clean, modern room and developed his prose style. 'Love is a money squandered thing.' 'In Spring a young man's fancy lightly turns to young men.' He fed into the typewriter the bits of old songs, captions, jingles, newspaper items, fan magazines, rhyming couplets, Hollywood clichés, glossy magazines, the compulsive dross his psyche battened on and mixed it all together with an energy that made it his own. Rejection slips rained in from editors and TV producers. To earn some money he got a job working night shifts at a pykelet-packing factory. Pykelets are a type of crumpet. 'He liked going out of the door at night wearing these huge overalls and carrying a flask of tea,' his mother said. 'He seemed to find that humorous.'

But his lust for fame remained. He subscribed to *Ritz*, David Bailey and David Litchfield's café society newspaper, and devoured its party coverage greedily. Joan Collins, Viviane Ventura, Victor Lowndes, Susan George, these were the giants of the Fleet Street columns, but now in the pages of *Ritz* he saw there were also others, a million others, boogeying through the newsprint in capital letters. He saw that fame was instantaneous simply by exposure. It was the electric current he'd dreamed of and he couldn't wait to wire up and live.

It was 1978 and café society had never been more Maxwell House. Bianca Jagger could still get away with being mysterious. Dai Llewellyn had not quite reached the end of his address book, and at a club, now defunct, called J. Arthur's in the New King's Road, pensioned-off Sex Pistols lolled on Dralon sofas. It was the disco era of poppers and Donna Summer and dancing on your own in a swirling gloom of mocca and mirrors and under-lit perspex. The recession had begun to bite but everyone believed nightlife had been saved by the Arabs. There was a wave of openings. Régine's was on its way with the promise of a million launch parties (it died last

---

Opposite: Party pack: *Frances O'F. dressed to thrill; fun person Timothy S. can't stop the music; late-night line-up, left to right, Alan Davidson, Adam Helliker, John St Clair, Timothy S., Lillian Burns, Frances O'F. and Ricci Burns*

year). Two more clubs opened that April — the Embassy under the aegis of recycled shirt-maker Michael Fish (now in other hands), and Bennet with a garden designed by Roddy Llewellyn (now closed). Gossip columns sang of the coming of Studio 54 (it never came), of fun places called Legend's (frontman: 'I can't stand superswish people') and The Alley (frontman: 'The decor will be Hollywood meets Somerset Maugham'). Maunkberry's in Jermyn Street was keeping its end up with smoked glass and smoked salmon but its

Rosie Boot's Guide to London Bachelors

Baron Steven Bentinck

There's still a few bob left in Baron Steven Bentinck. He only blew 200-odd grand on *Boulevard* and *Dean*. If that's made a dent in the fortune left him by his father Baron Adolph, the Dutch ambassador to London, his mother, Baroness Gaby is a Thyssen with her own pile to pass on. The certainty of stage two of the Bentinck inheritance is guaranted only since the departure from his life of explaymate of the month Marilyn Cole. She had just begun to put the breeze up his mother when her kiss-and-tell memoirs in the *Daily Mirror* made her, even in Steven's eyes, a busted flush.

Bentinck is now to be found running his own media packaging company in Sloane Street. It's called Legion. Because they are ten? 'No, twelve actually,' says Bentinck. 'And everyone of them's got *drive*.' To date, Legion have discovered a pop group called Ginger and made a short feature film about a nineteenth-century music-hall artist who farted his way through the Marseillaise.

Bentinck has come through his financial baptism of fire a new man. At 24, he looks 40. Moreover the acquisition of a ranch in Northern California has transformed him in the space of a year from a Bertie Wooster to J.R. Ewing. He has grown a mean moustache and walks with his Levi's slung low. 'I'm interested in people who want to be a *success*,' he told me. 'And are prepared to *work* for it. There are a helluva lot of people looking for *glamour* but not many people with *drive*.' To demonstrate the difference he flicked on a video cassette of his pop discovery Ginger. A well thatched lead singer made a pleasant Beatly noise while Bentinck swivelled triumphantly in his executive chair.

The nicest thing about Bentinck is his lasting commitment to spending his own money. He regrets none of his investments. He *believed* in *Dean* and he *believed* in *Boulevard*. Plainly it was not his fault that the press turned *Dean* into a comic fiasco and that his magazine, *Boulevard*, fell into the clutches of up-market motor-cycle freaks and free-associating leather fetishists. 'A lot of people have walked into this office with the wrong impression,' he said dankly. 'They think "He's young, rich and titled, he's *got* to be stupid".'

A pox on Marilyn Cole who opened the baby baron's eyes! She's made it much harder for all of us, but not, I assure you, impossible. Bentinck is still a sitting duck for a curvaceous management consultant. Dazzle him with your dossier, girls, and *then* take off your glasses . . .

manager reaffirmed its class in the face of all the new competition: 'It's like being in your own lounge,' he said. 'You don't feel that because someone's next to you in satin shorts you've got to pinch his arse.'

With the clubs came the promotion parties to fill them and with the parties a race of new guests whose faces fed the magazines. Under the inspiration of a bald pixie called Jeffrey Lane, the Rogers & Cowan public relations agency seemed to launch a fresh gravy train every night. The paparazzo Richard Young made anyone and everyone famous, including himself. It was the explosion of the B-list, the cult of wall-to-wall nobody, the ten o'clock crowd whose after-dinner breath never matched the host's. They formed a frenzied new society of their own, sparking off their own circuits.

Jordan, 'the first punk', was one of its celebrities. She had shot to fame by commuting from Brighton every day to her job at the King's Road shop called Sex wearing see-through ripped stockings with leather suspenders, see-through knickers, a ripped T-shirt and white bouffant hair. In the course of the next two years she did nearly 2,000 interviews on the subject of her appearance, starting with a full-splits shot in rubber for the first issue of *Ritz*. 'The media were definitely more receptive then,' she comments now. 'These days I think they expect more background.'

Quentin Crisp was rediscovered. For years he had been sitting in his room in the dust eating strawberry Complan and pronouncing on style. Now he was at the top of every PR's mailing-list. 'I have no idea why,' he told me in New York, whence he has since moved his bedsitting-room. 'I remember being especially surprised to be invited to Mr Travolta's party for the opening of *Saturday Night Fever* at a club whose name I forget in the Charing Cross Road. I did not know Mr Travolta personally. Nor do I know who, on that occasion, was the host. Perhaps London, for a minute, thought it was New York. Here promotional parties for 500 stangers are the norm. They all seem to take place on board a doomed liner. Lights flash but no help comes. That was rather the atmosphere at Mr Travolta's party, which was decidedly odd really for London.'

Timothy Swallow didn't find it odd. He found it wonderful. He met Quentin Crisp through Jordan, who'd got into conversation with him when he came up from Doncaster to visit the Sex shop in search of rubber trousers. Now he used Crisp to launch himself. Crisp introduced him to Robert T. Prior, the publisher of a gay magazine called *Gold*, which needed a gossip columnist. For a year Timothy hitch-hiked to London from Doncaster, working in the pykelet factory all week and covering the demi-monde at weekends. Splashed between spread after spread of glowering male genitals the columns were a vivacious read.

'Whirling my dervishes in time to the music I spun over to Billy's club in deplorable Soho,' ran one.

'Having failed to squeeze a second glass of Moët et Chandon from the pustular waiter I was cornered by the manager who told me one of his illustrious West End star guests would do her party trick and urinate into the glass. "At least it's cheaper than the house red," I replied soberly and it was on on on to the fab precincts of the Embassy Club.'

Gold was not the only magazine owned by Robert Prior. It was one of a clutch of titles that included *Adventure Sport*, *Hot Shoe* (a photographer's magazine) and *Bounce*, a magazine for women with busts over 40 inches. He ran his empire (and still does) out of three crepuscular rooms in South Molton Street, aided by his girlfriend, Penny Foulkes, a warm-hearted romp who writes and edits under a battery of male pseudonyms. When Timothy joined *Gold*, the other resident member of the team was the switchboard operator, Frances O'Farrell, then 23. Much of her day was spent fielding obscene phone calls from men who misunderstood the editorial message of *Bounce*. 'One man kept ringing up and asking me to put my breast into the receiver.' She and Timothy were immediately drawn to each other. Like him she had escaped from a small town background.

Her father worked for the GPO in Ruislip and Frances had gone to a convent in Cheltenham. She was not conventionally pretty but, as Dai Llewellyn puts it, 'Frances had a message'. The message came across loud and clear as she plunged around the fringes of fashion with her plump mouth and short, spiky hair. Only the large, opaque eyes differentiated her expectations of life from Timothy's, but the difference was crucial. She craved everything he craved, but without his irony.

They became inseparable. Using the magazine as their vehicle they went to everything — clubs, openings, book launches, scent launches, fashion shows, record promotions, anything that wanted hype. 'They were like Eckel and Peckel those two,' hairdresser Ricci Burns remembered, 'two kids from Noddyland out to play. They never knew when to say good night.' They became experienced gate-crashers, conning their way into functions they didn't have invitations for, often with one of *Gold*'s photographers, John St Clair, who became Timothy's best friend. St Clair, a pastel version of Christopher Reeve, had met Timothy when St Clair had squired David Hockney to the premiere of *Saturday Night Fever*. From then on Frances or Timothy always rang him the instant they heard of a new function to crash. 'I'd get myself in saying I was writing for *Frizz*,' St Clair told me. 'We'd drink a lot of free champagne and sit there slagging everybody off.' One of their greatest coups was penetrating a black-tie reception at Harrods where Timothy mingled unmolested in his rubber trousers then ate a three-course dinner serenaded by a string quartet.

They rowed a lot, Frances and Timothy. Frances enjoyed making Timothy jealous then taunting him that he was gay. He got his revenge by showing her up socially. They shacked up in Frances's bedsit in Kensington. At home he was fastidiously tidy, she compulsively chaotic. 'Anything could set them off,' Ricci said. 'Frances would spill a drink over his new trousers then, well, forget it. They'd still be shouting at two o'clock in the morning. It was all very Scott and Zelda.'

Nonetheless they were inordinately proud of each other. Timothy never ceased to be impressed by Frances's sexual flair. His photograph album celebrates her cleavage on every page. He encouraged her to vamp up in theatrical make-up and often spoke of her filmstar looks. Frances loved Timothy's puns. They made her feel sophisticated. She loved to hear his verbal joustings with Dai Llewellyn when they went on for a nightcap at Tokyo Joe's. His over-excitement always culminating in a rush of word-play. Then he'd hit the dance floor, punning wildly, his leathered legs going like pistons.

When *Gold* folded, Prior thought that the social explosion of clubs and promotion parties merited a new magazine, a 'sophisticated glossy' he called *London Index*. He made Swallow the editor. 'The timing seemed right,' Prior said. 'There seemed to be a lot of money about. And Timothy was ready for the break. He was put in the position where he could meet Joan Collins and he took to it.' Frances moved off the switchboard and did all the listings of clubs and hairdressers. She wrote a piece called 'The Glitter Girls' marvelling at the life of Mynah Bird and signing it off with a photograph of herself in Fifties sunglasses with the caption 'Our own glitter girl Frances O'Farrell'.

'Until people started to know me for myself I always went as Timothy's plus one,' she told me. 'The invitations got easier when he moved from *Gold* onto *Index*. He got on to everyone's list then. But sometimes he could only get one invite and went on his own. One night he came back with a lot of silver balloons for Régine's pre-launch party. Not the launch party the pre-launch party. He was very proud to have got into that.'

They moved again. 'We learnt,' Beryl Swallow said, 'always to write Timothy's phone number down in pencil.' This time their address had the right aura of stardom. The flat — in Islington — belonged to David Bowie's wife Angie, who'd lived there for a time with a failed rock star called Drue Blood. The walls were all decorated with signed Bowie photographs, the cupboards stuffed with his old costumes. Frances and Timothy often raided the cupboard when they went out or just spent the evening dressing up.

'People think we just went to parties,' Frances told me, 'but it isn't fair. We had lots of other interests. For instance, I've always been very interested in pathology and ballistics. It's very important sometimes if you're following a murder case to know which way the bullet went in. I got very interested in the Ripper case. We queued very early one morning so we could see the trial. Timothy thought Sutcliffe was mad. I thought he was evil. We sometimes used to ring up that number in the North and listen to the tape of the man who said he was the Ripper. Timothy was convinced it was someone he knew in Doncaster. Then every Saturday we'd try a new restaurant, Overton's one week. Carrier's the next. So you see, we did have our private world which we did enjoy and which Timothy rarely spoke about to others.'

London Index folded on its sixth issue. The thought of it still makes Bob Prior's panda eyes look sad. 'There just wasn't the market,' he explains. Frances went off to work as PR to Ricci Burns, but Timothy got his golden knock. There was a vacancy on Nigel

Dempster's column. 'He turned up for his interview in electric blue skin-tight trousers and a leopard-skin jacket,' Dempster's assistant Wendy Hussey remembered. 'We all knew from the moment he arrived that he was going to make his mark.'

He hated doing research for stories about some duke selling his stud farm but he loved doing his purple paragraphs about openings or film stars. 'He had a thing about star quality,' Wendy said. 'He once went to a première where he saw Liz Taylor and he said he nearly passed out on the pavement from sheer excitement.' Dirt-digging bored him but he took it in his stride. 'He liked taking people to the cleaners who were in the limelight,' Beryl Swallow said approvingly. 'We always said poison comes in little bottles. He used to say, that's right.' Timothy admired Nigel Dempster himself, or Caligula as he called him. He enjoyed his wit and smarted under his professionalism. Dempster in turn appreciated the delinquent drive of his new assistant, even if he had to rewrite Timothy's irrepressible touches of mauve. It seemed a perfect career step for a 25-year-old celebrity hound.

But there were problems. The difference between serious copy-getting and inventing a world in which he could star made Timothy tired. He could get into anything he liked now but found he often didn't want to. He took every press trip abroad — one highlight was Dai Llewellyn's freebie to Tunisia — but it was losing its thrill. While Frances flashed between Stringfellow's and Joe Allen's on the arm of tint artists from Ricci Burns, Timothy learnt that these places and these people came very low on the Mail Diary's hierarchy of glamour. He found himself having to rubbish what he'd previously revelled in. He accepted the toning-down of his appearance. 'He went from total punk to man-about-town,' Ricci Burns said. 'By the time he died he was Monsieur Classique.'

It is a sign of growing inner sobriety that after two years with Nigel he let himself be poached by the rival William Hickey column on the *Daily Express*. He had merely crossed the street for more money, a move that lacked his usual careerist flair. He told friends he enjoyed the more organised life of the *Express*. In his free time he began launching himself as a radio personality, doing gossip letters for a Los Angeles station and a London spot for Radio 3D in Melbourne whose signature tune was 'England Swings Like a Pendulum Do.'

He also started researching a biography of his old heroine, Bianca Jagger, and used the book as an excuse to take Frances to New York for the first time. They stayed at the Waldorf Astoria and ricocheted between Xenon, Studio 54 and four promotion parties a night. Timothy was particularly impressed by a party at Studio 54 for Andy Warhol and Brooke Shields where the party guests were

Rosie Boot's Guide to London Bachelors

The Hon Julian Hope

Now here's a man who needs a hard-headed woman. The Hon Julian Hope is crying out to be organised, if only you can be subtle about it. At 31 he has nothing left to lose — except his keys, his passport and his theatre tickets.

Hope, or Hopeless, as he is known afectionately to his girlfriends, is the eldest son of Lord Glendevon and Liza Maugham, Willie's daughter. He is a sturdy, preppy blond, with wavy but by no means curly hair. Preppiness, let it be said, has caught up with him rather than vice versa. He was wearing unstructured jackets and button-down shirts long before they were fashionable. He is quiet and vague and delightfully unraffish, qualities which more than make up for the fact that he always forgets to book a table. The jokes are there if you're prepared to wait for the first three gin and tonics. He goes at his own pace, formerly in a clapped-out Citroen.

If Hope is privately disorganised professionally he's a bit of a star, and would be more so if only he had a pushy wife to promote him. At Oxford, where he read English at Christchurch, he was the number one undergraduate opera producer. He caused a stir at the Edinburgh Festival in 1972 with *The Dissolute Punished*, Stephen Oliver's respectful perversion of Mozart's *Don Giovanni*. Since then he was worked at the Welsh National Opera, Glyndebourne and the wildly prestigious Wexford Festival. More recently he risked seeming less serious by taking on the out-of-town production of *The Rocky Horror Show* after a tennis game with Michael White. He was a bit hoity-toity about doing this and anxious to assure friends that he hadn't 'sold out'. But it's done wonders for his bank balance and got him to L.A., where his diffident charm has been a hit with West Coast music buffs.

In fact, in his quiet way Hope is a hit all round. For some time he courted the tempestuous beauty Mary Furness. Indeed, it was through her good offices that he finally lost his driving licence. Driving her home one night, she boisterously insisted on standing up with her head through the sunshine roof, which did not amuse the breathalysing patrol car behind.

Next he tried his luck with Miranda Guinness, but that romance bombed when he invited her to the Wexford Opera Festival. But there are hosts of other admirers willing to be cultured.

Home is a crepuscular mansion-block flat in Wetherby Gardens, which until recently he shared with ballgown baron Tom Bell, or his parents' tasteful house in the grounds of the Earl of Pembroke's place, Wilton House. Life would always be musical, if chaotic. But no arias, please. Even though Julian is attracted to prima donnas it's a backer he needs, and remember, when the going gets tough, the way to his handle is Handel.

divided off from the rest of the disco by a transparent veil. In the early hours the veil was lifted and the celebrities were suddenly sharing the same air as The Others. Frances noticed that as the trip wore on he seemed to have forgotten all about Bianca Jagger. Together they cruised singles bars. He had abandoned himself to the 'terminal thrill' of New York with Frances gyrating in his wake. 'He was full of New York when he came back,' Ricci Burns said. 'He kept on going on about "twinkettes" — pretty New York boys. D'you know it was Timothy who started the *Mommie Dearest* cult? He was the first one to take a coat-hanger into the cinema with him!'

In fact Timothy couldn't handle New York at all. John St Clair believes that the trip was a prelude to what happened six months later in Australia. 'He took too many pills,' St Clair said. 'Met too many weird people. Got up to too many weird things.' London had been his goal but now he saw that, compared to New York, London was as quiet as Doncaster. His identity fractured in a sea of jostling clones. Faced with all his fantasies of escape, he tasted the belittling nature of freedom. When he went home for Christmas he insisted on attending midnight mass. Frances refused so he took Jane Polden and they got stuck in a snowdrift for three hours coming home. 'He said it was the best time he'd had all year,' Jane said.

His mother was against him going to Australia in April last year to promote his radio appearances there. 'It was too far,' she told me. 'He wasn't practical enough to travel so far.' Two days before he left he rang an old friend from the church group, Andrew Mackenzie, with whom he'd had dinner only the week before. He asked if he could come and tell him something very important'. Andrew was busy. He never saw Timothy again.

What happened to Timothy and Frances in Australia? It was another round of press receptions and parties which Frances adored. They were put up in style at the Wentworth Hotel and Timothy discovered he was a minor star. According to Frances the last big fun time they had was at the screening of the Oscars one lunchtime. 'We behaved like mad poms and got very drunk on champagne,' she said. And yet Timothy had already been to an Australian doctor and acquired his fatal ration of pills.

He mixed them with alcohol sometime between midday and 3 p.m. on April 18th. Frances had not been back to the Wentworth all night. A boy had been in Timothy's room until noon. Frances had phoned the room repeatedly through the lunch hour. Finally one of the hotel staff broke in and found Timothy. 'I didn't realise how famous he had become in Australia until I saw all the papers,' Frances said. The coroner returned an open verdict.

'I want to be professionally me,' he had told me three months before he died, when I asked him his ambition. 'Just a name that doesn't have to be described with a job after it. I want to be like Andy Warhol — a big beautiful cloud. You put your hand into it and there's absolutely nothing.' He thought of fame not as a reward for achievement, nor even as an agent for material change, but as a state of being in itself that would free him at last from the demanding clutter of class, height and sex. Yet as he approached that state the clutter persisted. The weightlessness he dreamed of seemed not an escape at all but a free-falling emptiness. The only things that were real now were the roots he always believed had impeded him; but he could not go back. He looked instead for his terminal thrill.

In London John St Clair organised a memorial service at the Fleet Street church of St Bride's. Nigel Dempster read the lesson from Ecclesiastes. Afterwards Dai Llewellyn took Beryl, Kenneth and Jeffrey Swallow on a tour of Timothy's favourite night spots — Wedgies, Tokyo Joe's, Legends, ending with a midnight dinner at Stringfellow's.

Quentin Crisp was surprised to hear of the death. 'Mr Swallow! Never!' he cried, but he too wondered aloud whether it had all happened because Timothy in his quest to be a beautiful cloud had felt the callings to become a 'real person'.

Two days after his death Jane Polden received a postcard from Melbourne featuring a scene from Australian wildlife. The message read: 'This is about as wild as it gets. Timothy.'

The party's over: *Timothy S. lost in the Wednesday Night Fever crowd at Legends disco*

TAITTINGER